W9-BLJ-944

ROLLING PRAIRIE COOKBOOK

Nancy O'Connor

Over 130 recipes
celebrating fresh produce

illustrations by Karen Kerney • forward by Laurel Robertson

Copyright © 1998 Nancy O'Connor

All rights reserved. No part of this book may be transmitted
or reproduced in any form by any means without written
permission from the publisher.

Published by:
Spring Wheat Nutrition Education Services
1198 N 700 RD
Lawrence, Kansas 66047
FAX (785) 331-0842

Cover design by Annie Tichenor
Illustrations by Karen Kerney
Photo of author by Rick Mitchell

ISBN 0-9667403-0-0

Printed in the United States of America

on recycled paper

For Jim, Gabe, and Isaac
for inspiring, supporting, and loving me

ACKNOWLEDGEMENTS

Many, many people stand behind me—a whole community of people. Starting with the eight family farms who feed the hundreds of subscribers to Rolling Prairie Farmers Alliance. Thanks to Wayne and Sandy, Paul J., Tim and Alison, Stu and Patti, Paul C., Bob and Joy, Mark and Julie, Lynn and Dan, for providing me with succulent raspberries and beautiful golden zucchinis, and taking care of the soil, and reconnecting all of us to our food source. Hundreds of Rolling Prairie customers took the leap to Community Supported Agriculture. It is with their support and encouragement that this book is brought into being. I thank you.

THE inspiration for *Rolling Prairie Cookbook* may have come from the Rolling Prairie Farmers Alliance but the actual work of putting a book together was supported by a much more intimate community, starting with my family. I could not have asked for more. Editing, analyzing, proofing. Doing dishes after I cooked four new recipes. Graciously sampling all the recipes, and being gentle with your critiques when they didn't turn out quite right. Tolerating, loving, supporting. Thank you Jim, Gabe, and Isaac—you are an incredible pit crew. Even though Karen Kerney doesn't live in Kansas I feel she is an important part of my community. Karen's beautiful illustrations connect her to anyone who has enjoyed a fingerling potato or a hot pepper. I am grateful our paths touched at just the right time. Her drawings are a gift to the book. Thank you Karen. And then for the work of creating a physical book—putting words to paper, creating tabs, inserting pages, and making graphic boxes. Good friend Amy Fields convinced us, in her usual genial manner, that we could do the layout ourselves. She got us started and made sure we were well on the way. Thank you Amy. Laurie Martin-Frydman stepped in when we decided to completely change the layout of the book after having entered all the text and graphics. Thanks Laurie for getting us through that difficult spot. Sharon Burch, in her nurturing manner, gently changed the direction of *Rolling Prairie Cookbook* by sharing all she had learned during the publication of her own book *Recognizing Health and Illness*. Thank you Sharon for being so generous and open. It was Sharon's suggestion that perhaps I ought to think about getting input on the book from someone I considered an "expert" in the field. An expert in the field of food? I immediately knew there was no one whose opinion I would value more than Laurel Robertson, author of *Laurel's Kitchen*. I sent Laurel a portion of the manuscript with a letter explaining the project. She responded quickly with a kind and enthusiastic letter. Yes, she would look at the manuscript and would be happy to write a forward. Thank you Laurel for your support of this work, but even more, for providing a clear, loving voice in all your writings. Michael Ableman, author of *From the Good Earth* and *On*

Good Land also provided encouragement for this book. Michael is a strong voice for sustainable agriculture and for the importance of reconnecting to the foods we eat. Thank you Michael. Lynn Byczynski is one of the Rolling Prairie growers, but more than that she is a friend, and an inspiration to me. Lynn has a knack for creating and realizing visions. Being around her, I get the feeling I could do anything—like publish a cookbook. And so I did. Thank you Lynn for providing the spark and always keeping it fueled. After all was put to paper, it became pretty clear that we needed lots of eyes to catch the mistakes we couldn't see. It was no surprise that dear friend Helen Martin stepped up to the task. Helen has been intimately involved in Rolling Prairie, having been a dependable assistant with Monday night samplings at Community Mercantile. No doubt, Helen has seen as many Rolling Prairie customers as I have. She has tried and critiqued dozens of recipes, washed dishes at the demo kitchen, proofed thousands of words—all with great kindness and humility. Thank you Helen. Bob Lewis, with his eye for perfection and precision, was invaluable as a proofreader. Indeed, he is an amazing father-in-law. Thank you (Grandpa) Bob. I can really count on my family, and in the eleventh hour Andy and Juda Lewis stepped up to help proof the last round of vegetables. Thanks Andy and Juda for your enthusiastic support of this project and for being such loving family. In my introductory sections for the herbs, fruits, and vegetables, I dare to mention scientific names. I rest easy knowing that Steve and Aagje Ashe have looked over this work. Thank you for proofing, with special attention to genus and species! Good-natured Kelly Little was another eleventh-hour player, rescanning drawings and helping with final little graphic needs. At some point, as I closed in on the work of the recipes, my attention turned to the cover. If *Rolling Prairie Cookbook* is to be judged by its cover, I am in good stead. Annie Tichenor created a beautiful face for this work. Always calm, and accommodating, Annie took my ideas and worked her computer magic to create a beautiful cover. It all looked so easy when she showed me cover options on the computer screen. Thanks Annie for your artistic contribution to this work.

IT took a community to write this cookbook. Again, thank you to all who helped me get this cookbook to the kitchen table.

FORWARD

THIS is the kind of book I passionately wish for all of us who cook. To have in hand fresh-from-the-vine watermelons and picked-that-day raspberries, and (yippee!) unbashed rhubarb—opal basil, (and licorice, and cinnamon!)—chives and bok choy and cilantro—and dill and parsley and sweet new potatoes—wonderful, wonderful, "beyond all hooping." To sign on the dotted line so they arrive every week—Santa Claus in July—to belong to a CSA—that's wise, also a little brave. Lucky the eater who feasts on these succulent delicacies. Lucky the cook who can peek into the bag, see a crowd of kohlrabi peering back, and not feel faint . . . *That* is where this book comes in: *Rolling Prairie* is not an ordinary cookbook. *Rolling Prairie knows what's in the bag.*

THE recipes, admonitions, tips, and suggestions in this book talk pure northeast Kansas. They call for corn and butterhead and carrots from the farms you know, fresh and in season. You hold in your hand magic to make a celebration of Here and Now. *It's in the bag.*

KNEELING in her tomato patch one day, Joan Dye Gussow, head of the Department of Nutrition Education at Columbia Teacher's College, bit into an enormous Old Flame tomato hot from the sun. It occurred to her, juice dripping off her elbow, that after so many years of trying to educate Americans to eating better, most of them aren't. She asked herself, why would anyone buy a twinkie when they could tooth into *this? They don't know what they're missing.*

LATER on, after thinking about it, Joan told me she realized that the one thing she has seen that does inform—and transforms—people's relationship to food, is subscribing to a CSA. University colleagues, walking out into a spring rain, no longer rant, "I just washed my car!" Instead, softly, "I wonder if it is raining on my farm." An old friend calls up, "Someone at my CSA gave me this great recipe for Colache, you gotta come on over and have lunch." And, often: "We would never have tried these things, but we couldn't bear to throw them out, and mostly, we end up really liking them. Even the kids do."

JOAN agrees with Robyn Van Enn, the woman who first brought CSA to this country, that it's really *Agriculture Supported Community.* I think it's the hope of the future.

Laurel Robertson
Tomales, California
September 8, 1998

Contents

Vegetables, continued

INTRODUCTION

THIS is more than a cookbook about vegetables. This is a book about eight small family farms in Northeast Kansas. The people on these farms: Wayne and Sandy, Paul J., Tim and Alison, Stu and Patti, Paul C., Bob and Joy, Mark and Julie, Lynn and Dan, have made a commitment to farming organically and sustainably. Five growing seasons ago, they joined together to form the Rolling Prairie Farmers Alliance. These growers work to provide a wide range of fresh produce to customers who buy directly from the Alliance on a weekly basis for the duration of the growing season—about 24 weeks here in Kansas.

OVER 350 households "subscribed" to the Rolling Prairie Farmers Alliance in the 1998 growing season. That's a lot of produce, and a big commitment—both on the part of the growers and also the Rolling Prairie customers. It's a relationship that is forming in communities all across the country. This relationship even has a formal name; Community Supported Agriculture, or CSA. What that really means is that people are becoming connected to the food they eat, and to the people who grow the food. Small-scale farmers can plant their crops with some marketing assurance, because CSA customers have agreed to support these farmers by buying their produce. CSA customers receive weekly bags or boxes of the very freshest, locally grown produce directly from the growers. That means, of course, there is no asking for strawberries in July or tomatoes in May (at least not here in Kansas). Part of supporting local agriculture is learning to eat with the seasons. It's learning to patiently wait for tomatoes to ripen, or corn to come on. Your patience will be rewarded with quality and taste like nothing you can buy in a supermarket. You just can't pick a tomato green, ship it halfway across the country, store it in refrigeration, and put it out on display for days, and have it taste anything like Lynn and Dan's golden plum tomatoes that were just picked this morning and driven ten miles into town this afternoon to end up in my bag of Rolling Prairie produce. Being involved in a CSA also means exploring new foods and learning to cook greens, and kohlrabi, and mizuna—even if you don't know what they are—because that is what's plentiful and in season. That's where I come in. And where the *Rolling Prairie Cookbook* has come from.

THE seeds for this cookbook were first planted five years ago when the Rolling Prairie Farmers Alliance asked me if I would be interested in putting together weekly sheets for the Rolling Prairie customers. The sheets, appropriately named "In the Bag", contain recipes and ideas on how to use the produce the customers receive in their bag each week. The farmers may have planted the seed for this cookbook, but it has been the Rolling Prairie customers who have nourished and grown this book over the last five years. During that time I have had the opportunity to speak, quite literally, with hundreds of Rolling Prairie customers who have taken my ideas and recipes into their kitchens. They trusted me to help them eat their vegetables. They rewarded me time and again with their enthusiasm and positive responses to the recipes. Our kitchens and our dinner tables were linked—a deep honor.

AND so, the *Rolling Prairie Cookbook* has been created, with input from both the Rolling Prairie growers and customers. The fifty fruits, herbs, and vegetables represented in this book were chosen by the growers. It is not meant to be a comprehensive list of all that is grown in our part of the country. It is representative of what most often appears in the bags of produce distributed to Rolling Prairie customers. There are all sorts of other goodies that find their way into the bags—delectables like green soybeans, pea greens, and okra will just have to wait for the next cookbook. Each week of the growing season, for the past five years, I have sampled one of the weekly recipes to the customers at the pick-up site at Community Mercantile Co-op in Lawrence, Kansas. This means I am in the unique position of having hundreds of taste-testers to help me. I can say with assurance, the recipes in this cookbook are most definitely tried and true.

NOW having explained the deep roots of this cookbook, I would just like to say a bit more about the heart of this work. Each recipe was created to give a specific vegetable, fruit, or herb, an opportunity to shine. Some vegetables, like fresh corn on the cob, know how to take center stage very easily. Tomatoes also know how to hold their own. Kohlrabi, arugula, green tomatoes, fresh rosemary—these took more thought and testing. Never was I disappointed. Each vegetable, fruit, and herb revealed its distinct and wonderful personality. Working with fresh produce—chopping, mincing, slicing—can be renewing and nourishing, for those who partake of the results, as well as for those who prepare the recipes.

THE recipes in this book are all vegetarian. I do include dairy, cheese, and eggs. This is how I cook and so it is what I offer to you. The recipes are all nutritionally analyzed because I feel it is important for you to have a point of reference when making decisions about what to cook. If I give you exact measurements of ingredients like oil and salt, and tell you how that translates to a serving size, you can make decisions about adjustments you want to make so that these recipes fit best into your diet.

SO, where to get the fresh produce to prepare these recipes? After all, not everyone has the opportunity to join a CSA. There are other places to connect with your food, most notably at your local farmers' market. Here you can buy your fresh basil, and pick up a healthy dose of community at the same time. Get to know the growers. Talk to them. Ask them about their farms. Find out how they grow their melons. Ask them to recommend a variety of apple for Gingered Apple Crisp, or a type of hot pepper for Salsa Nancita. Don't be afraid to ask questions. We're learning to reconnect with our food and this is part of the process. Seek out growers who are committed to farming organically and sustainably. These are people who care about the earth they work. There will be times, like in December in Kansas, when you have to head to the grocery store for your carrots and potatoes. You still have choices. You can look for and buy certified organic produce. You can eat lots of root crops and potatoes, bypassing foods that are overpriced because they're so incredibly out of season. You can choose to buy what is the freshest possible produce. You can eat simply.

MY HOPE is that this book will inspire you. To change. To buy a vegetable you've never eaten before. To support local and sustainable agriculture. To reconnect with your food. To nourish and nurture yourself and those you love. I am honored to be invited into your kitchen. I hope this book helps to sustain you in some small way.

Nancy O'Connor
Lawrence, Kansas
Fall 1998

Fruits

APPLES

APPLES are one of the most versatile and familiar fruits. Although there are over 7,500 varieties of apples, just eight varieties account for 80 percent of domestic apple production: Golden Delicious, Granny Smith, Jonathan, McIntosh, Red Delicious, Rome Beauty, Stayman, and York. There's nothing quite as good as a locally grown, tree-ripened apple in late summer or early fall. Earlier varieties are usually more tart—great for baking. A few popular varieties that are delicious out-of-hand eating include Braeburn (slightly tart and firm), Fuji (super crisp and juicy), Jonathan (an old favorite, versatile apple with great semisweet taste), and Golden Delicious (when fresh and locally grown this is a wonderfully sweet and delectable fruit).

HANDLING: Summer apples don't store well. They should be eaten soon after picking and are at their best used in pies, cakes, or to add flavor to vegetable dishes. Fall apples like Jonathan, Red and Golden Delicious, and McIntosh are great to eat out-of-hand and are also delicious for baking, cooking, and applesauce (especially good in combination with one another). There is no need to peel organically grown apples. Store apples in the refrigerator.

SIMPLE PREPARATION: Wash your apple well, hold it in your hand, and take a big bite. If you have an abundance of apples there is nothing like homemade applesauce. Simply peel apples, then cut slices or chunks down to the core. Cook apple pieces over medium heat with enough apple juice or water to prevent sticking. Stir often and lower heat when apples begin to soften. Continue cooking, stirring occasionally, until apples are fully soft. Sweetener or cinnamon can be added near the end of cooking, but for pure apple flavor add nothing. For less chunky applesauce, wash but don't peel apples and run the cooked sauce through a cone colander to remove skins and smooth it up. Babies love it and so will you!

Here's a homey apple dessert that combines chewy dried apricots with fresh apples.

Apple Apricot Crumble

½ cup dried apricots, chopped and soaked in boiling water to cover for ½ hour
4 cups chopped, peeled apples (a mixture of sweet and tart apples, 4 to 5 apples)
3 tablespoons apple juice concentrate
½ teaspoon cinnamon

Topping:
2 tablespoons melted butter or canola oil
2 tablespoons apple juice concentrate
2 tablespoons maple syrup
¼ cup turbinado sugar
½ cup whole wheat pastry flour
1 teaspoon baking powder
¼ teaspoon salt
½ teaspoon cinnamon
1 cup quick-cooking rolled oats

Preheat oven to 350°F. Drain apricots. Mix apricots with apples, along with apple juice concentrate and cinnamon. Place mixture in an oiled, 10-inch baking dish.
To make topping: Stir butter or oil, apple juice concentrate, maple syrup, and sugar together. When well blended, sift in flour, baking powder, salt, and cinnamon. Mix well. Finally, work in the oats to form a stiff topping. Sprinkle evenly over fruit and bake for 45 minutes, or until apples are tender. Serves 8.

Nutrition information per serving, 8 servings per recipe: Calories: 199. Protein: 3g. Total fat: 4.1g (sat. fat: <1g). Carbohydrates: 37g. Cholesterol: 0mg. Sodium: 193mg. Vitamin A: 13% DV. Vitamin C: 5% DV.

Here's a lovely apple crisp—wonderfully spicy and not too sweet. Perfect served warm on a cool fall evening. A dollop of vanilla frozen yogurt perfectly balances the heat of the ginger.

Gingered Apple Crisp

8 cups sliced, peeled apples (8 to 10 apples)
½ cup liquid fruit concentrate or undiluted apple juice concentrate
¼ teaspoon ground nutmeg
1 teaspoon freshly grated ginger root

Topping:
5 tablespoons melted butter
¼ cup turbinado or brown sugar
1 teaspoon cinnamon
¼ teaspoon ground ginger
¼ teaspoon salt
1 cup crushed gingersnaps
2 cups quick-cooking rolled oats

Preheat oven to 350°F. Place apple slices in an unoiled 9 x 13-inch baking dish. Heat fruit or apple juice concentrate and grated ginger root in a small pan over medium heat until just simmering, about 5 minutes. Pour this liquid over the apples and stir to evenly distribute. Smooth apple filling evenly in pan. Mix remaining ingredients thoroughly to create topping. Cover apples evenly with topping. Bake for 40 to 45 minutes, or until apples are tender and topping is nicely browned. Serves 8 to 10.

Nutrition information per serving, 8 servings per recipe: Calories: 340. Protein: 4g. Total fat: 11.3g (sat. fat: 5.6g). Carbohydrates: 54g. Cholesterol: 21mg. Sodium: 190mg. Vitamin A: 8% DV. Vitamin C: 11% DV.

This is a simple cake—quick to make, moist with chunks of apple, great to pack in your lunch or grab as a quick snack on the way out the door.

Humble Apple Cake

6 tablespoons oil
½ cup honey
1 whole egg or 2 egg whites
1 teaspoon vanilla
½ cup buttermilk
1¾ cups whole wheat pastry flour (or a combination of whole wheat pastry flour and unbleached white flour)
½ teaspoon baking soda
½ teaspoon baking powder
¼ teaspoon salt
1½ cups chopped, unpeeled apples
½ cup chopped walnuts or pecans (optional)

Preheat oven to 350°F. Combine oil and honey. Beat in eggs, vanilla, and buttermilk. Sift in flour, baking soda, baking powder, and salt. Mix well. Stir in apples (and nuts if you're using them). Place mixture in a 7½ x 12-inch oiled pan and bake for approximately 35 minutes. Serves 12.

Nutrition information per serving, 12 servings per recipe, prepared with walnuts: Calories: 213. Protein: 4g. Total fat: 10g (sat. fat: 1g). Carbohydrates: 26g. Cholesterol: 14mg. Sodium: 113mg. Vitamin A: 1% DV. Vitamin C: 2% DV.

NUTRITION INFORMATION PER APPLE, 2¾" DIAMETER, RAW:

Calories: 81
Total fat: <0.3g
    (saturated fat: <0.2g)
Fiber: 4g
Sodium: 1mg
Potassium: 5% Daily Value
Vitamin A: <1% Daily Value
Vitamin C: 13% Daily Value
Iron: 2% Daily Value
Calcium: 1% Daily Value

APPLES

MELONS, squashes, and cucumbers are related. That sweet juicy watermelon may seem quite different from hard shelled winter squash, but home gardeners know that as members of the Cucurbitaceae family they all grow on vines. Most melons had roots in the Near East and eventually spread throughout Europe. There is evidence that the ancient Egyptians enjoyed the melons we know as cantaloupe. Columbus did his part to spread melons, carrying the seeds on his journeys around the world. Watermelon is botanically different from other melons and comes to us from Africa, where it originated in the desert. It was cultivated in Egypt as early as 2500 B.C. and was important because of its high water content. The traditional image of watermelon is that of a large fruit with a dark-green shell, red flesh, and lots of seeds. This is changing. Watermelons now also come in little round seedless varieties with flesh that can be buttery yellow, bright orange, or traditional red.

HANDLING: Whole melons should be kept at room temperature until they are ripe. Determining when they are perfectly ripe and ready to cut into is the real trick. Once you cut into a melon there is no turning back. It must now be eaten and the leftovers refrigerated. Cantaloupes have no green in the outer skin when they are fully ripe. The stem end will give just a little when light pressure is applied, and you should detect a faint smell of ripe melon. Honeydew's green outer skin should have a slightly yellowish cast when ripe and, like cantaloupe, the stem end should give slightly, with a sweet smell of honeydew. Watermelons can be a little more difficult to judge. If you purchase cut watermelon, your job is easier. Look for firm flesh, not watery, with deep color. When purchasing whole melons, I use the thumping method. Ripe melons should have a hollow sound when tapped.

SIMPLE PREPARATION: For cantaloupe and honeydew, cut fruit in half and scoop out the seeds. Using a paring knife, trim away the outer rind. Cut into bite-size pieces and serve. Or dice and mix with other seasonal fruits for a simple and welcome dessert—no need to add sweetener or embellishment. Watermelon—you know what to do.

It's been awhile since our family has been to Mexico but I still have memories of wonderful fruit drinks served up from small stands on the plazas of small towns and large cities. Melons work very well in these drinks, particularly sweet, juicy watermelons. Here are two variations to enjoy on a hot summer afternoon.

Watermelon Lemonade with Berries

2 cups seeded, cold watermelon chunks
½ cup frozen raspberries or strawberries
½ cup chilled lemonade
1 to 2 tablespoons sugar or honey (to taste)
8 to 10 ice cubes

Place all ingredients in a blender and whir until well blended. Pour into large, frosty mugs. Serves 2.

Nutrition information per serving, 2 servings per recipe: Calories: 130. Protein: 1g. Total fat: <1g (sat. fat: <1g). Carbohydrates: 30g. Cholesterol: 0mg. Sodium: 8mg. Vitamin A: 6% DV. Vitamin C: 42% DV.

Frosty Cantaloupe Smoothie

2 cups cantaloupe chunks
1 cup orange juice
2 tablespoons sugar or honey
8 ice cubes

Place all ingredients in a blender and whir until well blended. Pour into large, frosty mugs. Serves 2.

Nutrition information per serving, 2 servings per recipe: Calories: 157. Protein: 2g. Total fat: <1g (sat. fat: 0g). Carbohydrates: 36g. Cholesterol: 0mg. Sodium: 15mg. Vitamin A: 54% DV. Vitamin C: 217% DV.

This beautiful salsa is a nice departure from standard tomato-based salsas. It is a wonderful blend of hot and sweet—light, refreshing, and absolutely delicious. It will turn the most basic bean and rice meal into something special.

Sweet Melon Salsa

1½ cups finely chopped cantaloupe
1 shallot, minced
½ large green pepper, finely chopped
1 tablespoon minced fresh cilantro
1 or 2 hot peppers, seeded, and finely minced
 juice of 1 lime (approximately 3 tablespoons)
1 teaspoon honey, turbinado, or brown sugar
¼ teaspoon salt

Combine all ingredients. Refrigerate for at least half an hour to allow flavors to blend. Yield: 2 cups.

Nutrition information per 2 tablespoons: Calories: 10. Protein: 0g. Total fat: <1g (sat. fat: 0g). Carbohydrates: 2g. Cholesterol: 0mg. Sodium: 35mg. Vitamin A: 5% DV. Vitamin C: 22% DV.

NUTRITION INFORMATION PER ½ CUP MELON, RAW:

CANTALOUPE:
Calories: 29
Total fat: <0.2g
    (saturated fat: 0g)
Fiber: 0.6g
Sodium: 7mg
Potassium: 7% Daily Value
Vitamin A: 26% Daily Value
Vitamin C: 57% Daily Value
Iron: 1% Daily Value
Calcium: <1% Daily Value

WATERMELON:
Calories: 25
Total fat: <0.2g
    (saturated fat: <0.2g)
Fiber: 0.3g
Sodium: 2mg
Potassium: 3% Daily Value
Vitamin A: 3% Daily Value
Vitamin C: 13% Daily Value
Iron: 1% Daily Value
Calcium: <1% Daily Value

RASPBERRIES

RASPBERRIES

RASPBERRIES are a seasonal delicacy. When picked from their thorny canes, raspberries lose their core, making them extremely fragile. A member of the rose family, red raspberries first appeared in this country in the early seventeenth century, their origin most likely being Asian. We're most used to seeing red raspberries, but *Rubus idaeus* also comes in shades of deep purple, "black," and yellow—all with distinctive flavors. There is no better raspberry than a locally grown one.

HANDLING: With great care and as little as possible! Raspberries are probably one of the most perishable of all fruits. Eat them as soon after harvesting as possible. Rinse them very carefully if necessary. Raspberries freeze beautifully, so if you have surplus or can't eat your raspberries right away, consider freezing them for a wonderful treat later on. Spread raspberries out on a cookie sheet in a single layer and place in the freezer. When they are solidly frozen, place them in freezer bags.

SIMPLE PREPARATION: It feels like the ultimate luxury to be able to eat raspberries out of hand. There is no better way to enjoy their incredible flavor. If you only have a few, use them as embellishment, scattered on top of slices of ripe melon. If you have enough to make a pie or crisp, you are very lucky!

The name for this cake comes from it's appearance. The sweet cinnamon topping creates a very uneven, and very delicious, top crust—one of our family favorites.

Raspberry Wrinkle

¼ cup canola oil
½ cup honey
1 egg
½ cup lowfat or skim milk
2 cups whole wheat pastry flour
½ teaspoon salt
2 teaspoons baking powder
¾ teaspoon lemon zest
2 cups fresh raspberries (also wonderful with blueberries)

Crumb Topping:
¼ cup melted butter
⅓ cup turbinado or brown sugar
⅓ cup whole wheat pastry flour
½ teaspoon cinnamon

Preheat oven to 350°F. In a large bowl, blend together the oil, honey, egg, and milk. Sift the 2 cups of flour, salt, and baking powder and blend lightly into the wet ingredients. Carefully blend in the lemon zest and berries. Place mixture in an oiled 7½ x 12-inch baking pan. Mix topping ingredients together and drizzle over top of cake batter. Bake for approximately 45 minutes, or until cake is lightly browned and firm to the touch. Serves 12.

Nutrition information per piece, 12 pieces per cake: Calories: 229. Protein: 4g. Total fat: 8.8g (sat. fat: 2.9g). Carbohydrates: 33g. Cholesterol: 24mg. Sodium: 211mg. Vitamin A: 5% DV. Vitamin C: 9% DV.

Here is a good way to enjoy the taste of raspberries in a crisp without needing eight cups of precious berries. This crisp is a beautiful pale pink when baked. Delicious made with tart summer apples!

Apple Crisp with Raspberries

6 cups sliced apples (approximately 6 large apples)
2 cups fresh or frozen raspberries
¼ cup honey
1 tablespoon fresh lemon juice
1 teaspoon grated lemon zest

Crisp Topping:
½ cup whole wheat pastry flour
½ cup brown or turbinado sugar
1 cup quick-cooking rolled oats
1 teaspoon cinnamon
¼ teaspoon salt
⅓ cup cold butter

Preheat oven to 350°F. In a large bowl, toss the apples and raspberries with the honey, lemon juice, and lemon zest. Place fruit in an oiled 7½ x 12-inch baking pan. Combine flour, sugar, rolled oats, cinnamon, and salt in a medium-sized mixing bowl. Cut in the butter with a pastry cutter or two knives until mixture is the texture of coarse meal. Spread topping over apple mixture. Bake for approximately 50 minutes, or until apples are tender. Serves 8.

Nutrition information per serving, 8 servings per recipe: Calories: 253. Protein: 3g. Total fat: 8.2g (sat. fat: 4.8g). Carbohydrates: 41g. Cholesterol: 20mg. Sodium: 146mg. Vitamin A: 6% DV. Vitamin C: 23% DV.

The lovely taste of raspberries, when blended with peaches and hot peppers, yields this unique sweet (and gorgeous) salsa.

Raspberry Salsa

2 cups fresh raspberries
2 peaches, peeled and finely chopped
½ cup minced red onion
1 or 2 hot peppers, seeded and finely minced
juice of 1 lime
1 tablespoon red wine vinegar
1 teaspoon honey, turbinado, or brown sugar
¼ teaspoon salt

Combine all ingredients. Refrigerate for at least half an hour to allow flavors to blend. Makes about 2½ cups of salsa.

Nutrition information per 2 tablespoons: Calories: 28. Protein: 0g. Total fat: <1g (sat. fat: 0g). Carbohydrates: 6g. Cholesterol: 0mg. Sodium: 54mg. Vitamin A: 2% DV. Vitamin C: 37% DV.

NUTRITION INFORMATION PER ½ CUP RASPBERRIES, RAW:

Calories: 31
Total fat: <0.3g
    (saturated fat: 0g)
Fiber: 3g
Sodium: 0mg
Potassium: 3% Daily Value
Vitamin A: 1% Daily Value
Vitamin C: 26% Daily Value
Iron: 2% Daily Value
Calcium: 1% Daily Value

RASPBERRIES

RHUBARB

RHUBARB, or "pie plant" as it is sometimes called, is botanically a vegetable. The pinkish-green stalks may look somewhat like celery, but are never eaten raw. Rhubarb was cultivated by the ancient Chinese as early as 2700 B.C. for medicinal purposes. Edible rhubarb came along much later and didn't gain acceptance in this country until the 1800s. Rhubarb is a showy plant with large green leaves topping the edible stalks. Unfortunately, the beautiful leaves are poisonous and should be trimmed from the stalk and discarded. Rhubarb has a very tart personality that is complemented by that other springtime fruit—strawberries.

HANDLING: Rhubarb stalks should be firm. They can be greenish-pink to deep red. The thinner stalks are usually less stringy. Trim off any of the leaf that remains attached and discard this poisonous part of the plant. Stalks may be stored in a plastic bag in the refrigerator for up to a week. If you don't use your rhubarb right away, consider freezing it. Wash and dry the stalks, slice or chop, and store in freezer bags. No blanching is required.

SIMPLE PREPARATION: Stewed rhubarb is easy and versatile. It is a favorite at our house served as a topping for pancakes or waffles. It is also delicious mixed with yogurt. To stew rhubarb, combine 4 cups sliced rhubarb with approximately ½ cup sweetener (sugar, honey, or maple syrup), and ½ cup liquid (water, orange juice, or apple juice). Simmer over medium heat until rhubarb is tender and "saucy". Stir frequently to avoid scorching. Rhubarb can be cooked in combination with apples or strawberries to help tame its tartness. The addition of strawberries will make a thinner sauce.

This bread pudding, studded with bits of fresh rhubarb, is as good for breakfast as it is for dessert. It is especially delicious still warm with a small spoonful of vanilla ice cream or frozen yogurt (that is if you're eating it for dessert).

Rhubarb Bread Pudding

8 slices of bread, toasted*
2 cups skim milk
2 tablespoons butter
¾ cup honey
½ teaspoon vanilla
2 eggs, beaten
2 cups diced rhubarb (2 to 3 medium-sized stalks)
½ teaspoon cinnamon
¼ teaspoon salt

Topping:
2 tablespoons turbinado or brown sugar
2 tablespoons instant oatmeal
¼ teaspoon cinnamon
⅛ teaspoon grated nutmeg

Cut toast into cubes. Place in medium-sized buttered baking dish (approximately 2 quart). Scald milk. Add butter to milk and stir until melted. Stir honey and vanilla into milk. Pour milk mixture over bread cubes and allow to sit 15 minutes. Preheat oven to 325°F. Add eggs, rhubarb, cinnamon, and salt to bread mixture and stir carefully until well blended. Mix topping ingredients and sprinkle evenly over top of pudding. Bake, uncovered, for 45 to 50 minutes, or until pudding is firm and golden. Serves 8.

*This pudding is delicious made with Italian bread. It is light and almost creamy. I also prepare this recipe with whole wheat bread and it is equally good— a more hearty and earthy dish.

Nutrition information per serving, 8 servings per recipe: Calories: 270. Protein: 7g. Total fat: 4.4g (sat. fat: 2.4g). Carbohydrates: 49g. Cholesterol: 51mg. Sodium: 322mg. Vitamin A: 11% DV. Vitamin C: 5% DV.

RHUBARB

This cake is moist with rhubarb and buttermilk and subtly spiced with cinnamon and allspice.

Rhubarb Cake

2 cups flour (whole wheat pastry, unbleached white, or a combination)
1½ teaspoons baking powder
½ teaspoon baking soda
¾ teaspoon cinnamon
¼ teaspoon allspice
½ teaspoon salt
½ cup canola oil
½ cup honey
¼ cup turbinado or brown sugar
2 eggs, beaten
1 teaspoon vanilla extract
1 teaspoon orange zest
1 cup buttermilk
2 cups diced rhubarb

Preheat oven to 350°F. In a large bowl, mix oil, honey, sugar, eggs, vanilla, and orange zest. Sift in the flour, baking powder, baking soda, cinnamon, allspice and salt. Stir in the buttermilk. Finally, stir in the rhubarb. Pour cake batter into an oiled 7½ x 12-inch pan. Bake for approximately 35 minutes, or until cake is golden and firm to the touch. Serves 12.

Nutrition information per serving, 12 servings per recipe: Calories: 216. Protein: 5g. Total fat: 9.9g (sat. fat: 1.1g). Carbohydrates: 26g. Cholesterol: 28mg. Sodium: 191mg. Vitamin A: 3% DV. Vitamin C: 4% DV.

NUTRITION INFORMATION PER ½ CUP RHUBARB, RAW:

Calories: 13
Total fat: 0g
    (saturated fat: 0g)
Fiber: 1g
Sodium: 3mg
Potassium: 5% Daily Value
Vitamin A: 1% Daily Value
Vitamin C: 8% Daily Value
Iron: 1% Daily Value
Calcium: 5% Daily Value

RHUBARB

Herbs

BASIL

BASIL derives its name from the Greek word *basilicum,* meaning royal, kingly, or magnificent. Indeed, this member of the mint family is a magnificent herb. A slight bruise of a leaf releases a rich and spicy smell. There are over sixty varieties of basil, many cultivated for use in perfumes. Some of the more familiar culinary basils include lemon basil, cinnamon basil, licorice basil, and beautiful opal basil. This most fragrant herb is a natural companion to tomatoes, both in the garden and on the dinner table. There is no finer combination of tastes than a tomato fresh from the vine with a dab of homemade pesto.

HANDLING: Ideally, you would have a fresh pot or plot of basil that you could pick from whenever you needed a sprig or a handful. You would harvest your herbs early in the day when the plant was fresh and the energy and oils were up in the leaves. If you purchase fresh basil you need to take good care of it since it is quite perishable. Do not wash the leaves until you're ready to use them. Treat your basil like a bouquet of fresh flowers, placing the sprigs in a small jar of water out of direct sunlight. Basil sealed in a plastic bag in the refrigerator will turn brown quickly, especially if there is any water trapped inside the bag. Another way to preserve basil is to layer the leaves in a jar with olive oil. If you have a great quantity of basil, consider making several batches of pesto (recipe follows). Pesto can easily be frozen. Simply pack into containers and freeze. Or place mounds of pesto on a cookie sheet, freeze until solid, then remove and place in bags.

SIMPLE PREPARATION: Fresh basil leaves can be snipped with kitchen shears. Fresh basil is wonderful on pizzas, in omelets, on sandwiches, in tomato sauces, and in vegetable soups. When substituting fresh basil for dried in a recipe, use about three times the amount since fresh herbs are less concentrated than dried.

Pesto is most often served as a rich topping for pasta. Simply toss a small amount with hot pasta until evenly distributed. Pesto is also delicious on sandwiches. Wheatfields Bakery in Lawrence, Kansas, offers a pesto/goat cheese/roasted pepper/watercress sandwich on homebaked soft Italian bread that is absolutely wonderful. Try a variation of this sandwich substituting thick, fresh tomato slices for peppers. Pesto is also excellent added in small amounts to potato salad, soups, cold pasta salad, or in your favorite salad dressing.

Basic Pesto

2 cups lightly packed basil leaves (or a combination of basil and parsley)
2 to 4 cloves garlic
¼ cup pine nuts
¼ teaspoon salt
½ cup grated Parmesan cheese
¼ cup olive oil

Place basil, garlic, and pine nuts in a food processor*. Pulse until well blended. Add salt and cheese. Pulse again. While food processor is running, add oil in a steady stream. Allow to process until a thick, smooth paste is formed. Makes approximately 2 cups pesto.

*Pesto can also be made in a blender, but this will require more patience, and more starting and stopping. You may want to hand chop the herbs and garlic to help the process along. Also, you may want to start with a little oil in the bottom of the blender before you heap in the greens.

Nutrition information per ¼ cup : Calories: 110. Protein: 3g. Total fat: 9.9g (sat. fat: 2.2g). Carbohydrates: 1g. Cholesterol: 4mg. Sodium: 160mg. Vitamin A: 9% DV. Vitamin C: 6%DV.

Here's a recipe inspired by the wonderful cookbooks of Renee Shepherd and Fran Raboff, *Recipes from a Kitchen Garden* and *More Recipes from a Kitchen Garden*. These two cookbooks are an inspiration—coming from two women who obviously love gardening, and cooking what the garden has to offer.

Orzo and Zucchini with Pesto Dressing

1½ cups uncooked orzo (rice-shaped pasta)
2 medium zucchini, thinly sliced, then quartered (approximately 4 cups)*
1½ cups fresh basil leaves
3 tablespoons olive oil
½ cup grated Parmesan cheese
3 to 4 cloves garlic
½ teaspoon salt
black pepper to taste

Bring a large pot of water to a boil and cook orzo until just tender while you prepare the rest of this easy dish. Lightly steam zucchini slices until just barely tender. Rinse under cool water and drain well. (For an especially delicious flavor, you can grill long strips of zucchini, then cut into small slices.) Combine basil, olive oil, Parmesan, garlic, and salt in a food processor and whir until well blended. Drain cooked orzo and toss, while still warm, with cooked zucchini and basil dressing. Season with plenty of freshly ground black pepper. Serve immediately with thick slices of fresh tomatoes, corn on the cob, and soft Italian bread for a meal that celebrates summer. Cold leftovers are surprisingly good. Serves 6 to 8.

*This dish is even more attractive if you use one golden and one green zucchini.

Nutrition information per serving, 6 servings per recipe: Calories: 144. Protein: 5g. Total fat: 8.4g (sat. fat: 2.1g). Carbohydrates: 11g. Cholesterol: 5mg. Sodium: 305mg. Vitamin A: 4% DV. Vitamin C: 15% DV.

NUTRITION INFORMATION PER 2 TABLESPOONS BASIL, FRESH:

Calories: 1
Total fat: trace
        (saturated fat: trace)
Fiber: trace
Sodium: trace
Potassium: <1% Daily Value
Vitamin A: 4% Daily Value
Vitamin C: 3% Daily Value
Iron: 1% Daily Value
Calcium: 1% Daily Value

CHIVES

CHIVES in the garden are a sign of spring. They are one of the first herbs to reappear after a long winter. Chives are a member of the *Allium* genus, but unlike their onion and garlic relatives, chives don't produce an edible bulb—the only usable parts of the plant are the long, slender, hollow leaves. Chives produce a beautiful purple flower if they are allowed to bloom. For best flavor and production, it is best to snip the blossoms off the plant as they form. If chives do bloom, the flowers themselves are an attractive addition to a green salad.

HANDLING: As with any fresh herb, the ideal would be to have a pot of chives on your kitchen windowsill to snip when you need them. If you have a little bundle of fresh chives and you aren't going to use them right away, the best way to store them is in the freezer, where they will keep for up to three months and still have pretty good flavor. Freeze entire leaves, and when you're in need of chives, snip what you need of the frozen herb and place the rest back in the freezer.

SIMPLE PREPARATION: Just snip with kitchen shears. The flavor of chives is not enhanced by cooking, so it's best to add fresh chives right before your dish is served. Chives are well paired with eggs in omelets and savory custards. A snip of chives is the perfect garnish for a bowl of cream soup or in cream sauce. Soften butter and blend in chives to create a spread that's delicious on baked potatoes, corn on the cob, or grilled on a piece of crusty French bread.

This flavorful spread is especially good on thin rice crackers or toasted slices of baguette. For an impressive looking, and especially delicious appetizer, spoon several tablespoons of fresh pesto on top of Chived Chèvre Cheese before serving. Embellish with fresh basil leaves.

Chived Chèvre Cheese

1 cup Chèvre (mild, soft goat cheese)
1 cup reduced-fat cream cheese
¼ to ⅓ cup snipped fresh chives
2 to 4 tablespoons finely minced fresh parsley
2 to 4 tablespoons finely chopped fresh basil
freshly ground black pepper to taste

Cream Chèvre and cream cheese together until well blended. Add fresh herbs and continue to cream until thoroughly combined. Roll into a ball, place on a small serving plate, cover, and chill. Makes approximately 2½ cups of spread.

Nutrition information per ¼ cup: Calories: 129. Protein: 6g. Total fat: 10.4g (sat. fat: 6.8g). Carbohydrates: 2g. Cholesterol: 36mg. Sodium: 196mg. Vitamin A: 6% DV. Vitamin C: 2% DV.

To make delicious rice salad you need to use high quality rice that is carefully cooked. In this recipe, basmati rice contributes a subtle, flowery taste, complemented by fresh chives and basil.

Rice Salad with Chives

4 cups cooked basmati rice (either white or brown), cooled to room temperature*
1 carrot, coarsely grated
1 large yellow bell pepper, cut in thin slivers
1 cup fresh or frozen peas, just barely steamed
¼ cup snipped fresh chives
2 tablespoons finely chopped fresh basil
¼ cup olive oil
1 tablespoon fresh lemon juice
1 garlic clove, minced or pressed
¾ teaspoon salt
lots of freshly ground black pepper

Toss cooked rice with carrot, bell pepper, peas, chives, and basil. Whisk olive oil, lemon juice, and garlic together. Pour over rice mixture. Season with salt and pepper. Toss well. Chill for several hours. Toss again just before serving. Serve on a bed of lettuce with fresh tomato wedges on the side. Serves 8.

*Rinse your rice in cool water and drain well—for this recipe you'll need 2 cups uncooked rice. Pour 1 teaspoon of olive oil in the bottom of the saucepan that you'll use to cook the rice, and heat over medium-low heat. Add rice to the pan and stir well until all the rice kernels are evenly coated with oil, approximately 1 to 2 minutes (the rice will smell wonderful as it lightly toasts). Add 4 cups cool water. Turn heat to high. Bring to a full boil, and allow to boil for 3 minutes. Turn heat to low, cover, and cook until all the water is absorbed. It is important during this process that the rice is not stirred or you will end up with a sticky mass, rather than the individual kernels you want for a cold salad. To check for doneness, use a fork to carefully part the rice and check for water at the bottom of the pan. If there is still a little water, continue cooking until water is absorbed and rice is tender. White basmati takes approximately 15 minutes to cook, brown basmati takes approximately 45 minutes.

Nutrition information per serving, 8 servings per recipe: Calories: 184. Protein: 3g. Total fat: 6.8g (sat. fat: 1g). Carbohydrates: 27g. Cholesterol: 0mg. Sodium: 206mg. Vitamin A: 28% DV. Vitamin C: 28% DV.

Even if you're not much of a baker, give these savory biscuits a try. They are the perfect accompaniment to a pot of homemade soup or to add cheer to the kitchen on a cold winter day.

Cheddar Cheese Biscuits with Chives

2 cups flour (whole wheat pastry, unbleached white, or a combination of the two)
½ teaspoon salt
2½ teaspoons baking powder
½ teaspoon baking soda
¼ cup grated sharp Cheddar cheese
2 to 3 tablespoons finely chopped fresh chives
4 tablespoons cold butter
1 cup lowfat buttermilk
1 teaspoon honey or other sweetener

Preheat oven to 450°F. Sift flour, salt, baking powder, and baking soda into a medium-sized bowl. Add cheese and chives. Toss to evenly distribute. Cut butter into flour mixture using a pastry cutter or two knives. Mixture should resemble coarse meal. Mix buttermilk and sweetener together. Make a well in the middle of the flour mixture and pour in buttermilk. Stir quickly and lightly with a fork until mixture *just* comes together, approximately ½ minute—it is very important to not overwork the dough or your biscuits will be tough. Turn dough out onto a flat surface and very lightly knead until dough comes together (again, only about ½ minute). If you need to add a sprinkling of flour to help with kneading, that's fine. Pat dough out to a thickness of approximately ¾ inch. Cut biscuits with a 2-inch biscuit cutter or sharp knife. Whatever you use, make sure the edges of the biscuits aren't crimped or their wonderful rise in the oven will be hampered. Place on a lightly oiled cookie sheet. Bake for 12 to 15 minutes or until golden. Keep a watchful eye on the clock—these rich biscuits brown quickly. Serve hot! Makes approximately 20 biscuits.

Nutrition information per biscuit: Calories: 74. Protein: 3g. Total fat: 3g (sat. fat: 1.9g). Carbohydrates: 9g. Cholesterol: 8mg. Sodium: 175mg. Vitamin A: 2% DV. Vitamin C: 0% DV.

Here's the perfect dip to place in the center of a big, beautiful fresh vegetable platter.

Fresh Chive Dip

1½ cups lowfat sour cream
1½ cups yogurt
¼ cup finely minced fresh parsley
⅓ cup freshly snipped chives
¼ teaspoon salt
freshly ground black pepper to taste

Combine all ingredients. Chill for several hours to allow flavors to blend. Serve with an array of fresh garden vegetables. Makes approximately 3½ cups of dip.

Nutrition information per ¼ cup: Calories: 62. Protein: 2g. Total fat: 4.8g (sat. fat: 2.9g). Carbohydrates: 3g. Cholesterol: 10mg. Sodium: 87mg. Vitamin A: 5% DV. Vitamin C: 3% DV.

NUTRITION INFORMATION PER 2 TABLESPOONS CHIVES, FRESH:

Calories: 1
Total fat: trace
   (saturated fat: trace)
Fiber: trace
Sodium: trace
Potassium: <1% Daily Value
Vitamin A: 4% Daily Value
Vitamin C: 4% Daily Value
Iron: trace
Calcium: trace

CILANTRO

CILANTRO is a very perishable cut herb, which seems uncharacteristic considering its bold and assertive personality. Growing in the garden it is lovely—delicate leaves that look somewhat like the leaves of Columbine. Cilantro can't tolerate heat and soon puts out feathery leaves that precede its flowering stage. The seeds of fresh cilantro are coriander, *Coriandrum sativum,* so technically, cilantro is fresh coriander. Coriander was cultivated by the Egyptians and containers of the seeds have been found in royal tombs. The leaf of coriander was disdained by English and European herbalists, and no doubt some modern-day cooks as well, but it is a favored herb in the cuisines of Mexico, India, and Asia. It has a bright, earthy flavor that is incomparable in fresh summer salsa.

HANDLING: The leaves of cilantro wilt easily so treat your fresh herb carefully, like a little bouquet. Often cilantro comes bunched, with the root ends conveniently altogether. Sometimes the roots are still attached—so much the better. Place your cilantro bouquet in a small glass of water, cover loosely with plastic, and store in the refrigerator.

SIMPLE PREPARATION: If need be, rinse your cilantro leaves in cool water just before use to remove any dirt. Hand-pluck or trim leaves from the thicker stems using scissors or a sharp knife. Fresh cilantro is most often added in the last minutes of cooking or used as a final embellishment just before serving. The leaves are so delicate I find them difficult to chop and often just snip the leaves with scissors right into the dish in which I'm using the herb. Fresh cilantro is excellent in salsa and is equally wonderful in Indian rice dishes and raita (a cooling yogurt side dish). If you're not familiar with the power of fresh cilantro, it is best to start with a little and add more after you sample your recipe.

If you like cilantro, you'll love this extremely flavorful pesto. Its decidedly Southwestern personality is good with pasta and tasty with grilled vegetables, as an embellishment for enchiladas, or served with polenta.

Cilantro Pesto

 1 cup fresh cilantro leaves
 ½ cup fresh parsley leaves
 ½ cup fresh basil leaves
 2 garlic cloves
 1 mild hot pepper, roasted, peeled, and seeded (optional)
 ½ teaspoon salt
 ½ cup grated Parmesan or Asiago cheese
 2 to 3 tablespoons fresh lime juice
 4 tablespoons olive oil

Place cilantro, parsley, basil, garlic, and roasted pepper in a food processor*. Pulse until well blended. Add salt, cheese, and lime juice. Pulse again. While food processor is running, add oil in a steady stream. Allow to process until a thick, smooth paste is formed. Makes approximately 2 cups pesto.

*Pesto can also be made in a blender, but this will require more patience, and more starting and stopping. You may want to hand chop the herbs and garlic to help the process along. Also, you may want to start with a little oil or lime juice in the bottom of the blender before you heap in the greens.

Nutrition information per ¼ cup: Calories: 89. Protein: 2g. Total fat: 7.8g (sat. fat: 1.8g). Carbohydrates: 2g. Cholesterol: 4mg. Sodium: 229mg. Vitamin A: 4% DV. Vitamin C: 35% DV.

This colorful salad combines lots of wonderful summer flavors—it's filled with the freshness of herbs, the tang of lime, with a bit of fire from the hot pepper. For a fun meal, serve it with tortilla chips, wedges of garden tomatoes, light sour cream or grated Jack cheese, and salsa.

Festive Couscous Salad

1 cup couscous*, soaked in 1 cup boiling water, then cooled to room temperature
2 cups cooked black or kidney beans (rinsed and drained)
2 cups fresh or frozen corn kernels, lightly steamed
1 large carrot, diced
1 bell pepper, finely chopped (red, yellow, or green)
½ cup chopped green onions
1 fresh hot pepper, minced (more or less to taste)
¼ cup chopped fresh cilantro (more or less to taste)
¼ cup chopped fresh parsley
¼ cup chopped fresh basil
6 tablespoons olive oil
4 to 6 tablespoons fresh lime juice
3 cloves garlic, minced or pressed
¾ teaspoon ground cumin
¾ teaspoon salt
freshly ground black pepper to taste

In a large bowl, toss together the couscous, black beans, corn, carrot, bell pepper, green onions, and hot pepper. Sprinkle on the cilantro, parsley, and basil. Toss again until herbs are well distributed. Whisk or shake together the olive oil, lime juice, and garlic. Drizzle over salad. Season with cumin, salt, and pepper. Combine well. Refrigerate for several hours. Toss again before serving. Serves 8.

*Couscous is actually tiny pasta made from semolina wheat. Of North African origin, couscous is traditionally yellow colored. It is also available in whole wheat for a slightly heartier taste. The beauty of couscous is the ease with which it comes to life. Place 1 cup of couscous in a bowl, cover with 1 cup boiling water, cover, and allow to sit for 5 minutes. Fluff with a fork. If couscous is still a little crunchy, add several tablespoons more water and give it a few more minutes.

Nutrition information per serving, 8 servings per recipe: Calories: 216. Protein: 5g. Total fat: 9.7g (sat. fat: 1.4g). Carbohydrates: 26g. Cholesterol: 0mg. Sodium: 208mg. Vitamin A: 30% DV. Vitamin C: 48% DV.

Colache is a classic Mexican vegetable dish that combines corn and summer squash. It is a perfect light side dish to accompany hearty bean burritos. Or serve on a bed of basmati rice with a sprinkle of sharp Cheddar cheese, with warm corn tortillas to round out the meal.

Mexican Vegetable Medley (Colache)

2 tablespoons canola oil
2 cloves garlic, minced or pressed
1 small onion, chopped
3 or 4 small summer squash (any variety or color), cut in ¼ inch thick slices
1 red bell pepper, cut in matchsticks
2 cups corn kernels (fresh is best)
2 medium tomatoes, peeled and coarsely chopped
½ teaspoon salt
freshly ground black pepper to taste
¼ cup (or more to taste) chopped fresh cilantro

Heat oil in a large, deep skillet over medium heat. Add the garlic and onions. Sauté for 2 to 3 minutes. Add the squash and bell pepper. Sauté for another minute or two. Add corn and chopped tomatoes. Reduce heat to medium-low. Cover and simmer vegetables until just tender—approximately 5 minutes. If vegetables begin to stick, or mixture seems too dry, add a small amount of water. Season with salt and pepper. Toss in the cilantro. Serve immediately. Serves 6.

Nutrition information per serving, 6 servings per recipe: Calories: 109. Protein: 2g. Total fat: 4.8g (sat. fat: <1g). Carbohydrates: 14g. Cholesterol: 0mg. Sodium: 191mg. Vitamin A: 14% DV. Vitamin C: 66% DV.

NUTRITION INFORMATION PER 2 TABLESPOONS CILANTRO, FRESH:

Calories: <1
Total fat: 0g
    (saturated fat: 0g)
Fiber: trace
Sodium: <1mg
Potassium: <1% Daily Value
Vitamin A: <1% Daily Value
Vitamin C: 0% Daily Value
Iron: <1% Daily Value
Calcium: <1% Daily Value

CILANTRO

DILL is another herb, like cilantro, that has a split personality. The wispy leaves of dill weed provide a delicate, almost grassy taste—most commonly used in potato dishes. The seed of the dill plant is much bolder and is somewhat like caraway seed in taste. The common name "dill" is derived from the Saxon *dillan,* which means to lull or soothe. Romans chewed on dill seeds to promote digestion, babies in England, Europe, and Turkey were commonly given dill water to soothe their colic, and in the American colonies, restless children were given dill seeds to chew on during long church meetings.

HANDLING: Treat fresh dill weed like many of the other fresh herbs with stems. Place stalks in a small jar of water and store in your refrigerator. Use as soon as possible to retain the fresh flavor of this delicate herb. If you have more fresh dill than you can use, you can snip fresh dill weed directly into a small container that has a tight fitting lid and pop it right into your freezer. Use at a time when fresh herbs aren't available and you need your spirits uplifted.

SIMPLE PREPARATION: Get out your scissors and snip little bits of fresh dill weed into your green salad, scrambled eggs, omelets or quiches, potato salad, salad dressings, and cucumber salads. Dill weed has an affinity for cabbage—try it in slaw and soups made with cabbage. This light, springy-tasting herb is particularly wonderful in hot soups with a milk base.

This savory salad is a wonderful blend of flavors and textures. For those who have never explored lentils, this is a good place to start. This recipe comes from friend Nancy Smith, editor of *Back in Thyme*, a bimonthly newsletter about heirloom flowers, herbs, and plants.

Lentil and Feta Cheese Salad

1 cup raw lentils, sorted and washed
1 green pepper, chopped
2 ripe tomatoes, chopped
1 small onion, chopped
½ cup sliced black olives
½ pound Feta cheese, crumbled
¼ cup olive oil
juice of 1 lemon
2 tablespoons red wine vinegar
2 tablespoons fresh basil*
2 tablespoons fresh dill weed*
1 tablespoon fresh summer savory (or thyme or oregano)*
½ teaspoon salt
freshly ground black pepper to taste
lettuce and lemon wedges for garnish

Cover lentils with 3 cups water and bring to a boil. Lower heat and simmer until tender, about 30 minutes. Watch lentils toward end of cooking time so that they don't overcook. Cool cooked lentils, then mix with remaining ingredients. Refrigerate for 2 hours to allow flavors to mesh. Serve on a bed of lettuce and garnish with lemon wedges. Serves 8.

*When using dried herbs, substitute about 1 teaspoon dry for 1 tablespoon fresh.

Nutrition information per serving, 8 servings per recipe: Calories: 234. Protein: 9g. Total fat: 15g (sat. fat: 5.6g). Carbohydrates: 15g. Cholesterol: 25mg. Sodium: 566mg. Vitamin A: 13% DV. Vitamin C: 39% DV.

This is comfort food—at its best. Potatoes, cheese, and fresh herbs are baked together to create a friendly and familiar dish.

Au Gratin Potatoes with Fresh Dill

6 cups chopped, unpeeled potatoes, cut in ½ inch cubes
1 tablespoon olive oil
1 large onion, finely chopped
1 red bell pepper, finely chopped
⅓ cup minced fresh dill weed
⅓ cup minced fresh parsley
1½ cups reduced-fat Cheddar cheese, grated
1 cup reduced-fat sour cream or yogurt
½ cup skim milk
¾ teaspoon salt
freshly ground black pepper to taste
¾ cup dry bread crumbs

Lightly oil a large baking dish. Put on a large pot of water to boil the cubed potatoes. Cook the potatoes until just barely tender. Drain well and set aside. Preheat the oven to 350°F. Heat oil in a medium-sized skillet over medium heat. Add the onion and red pepper. Sauté for approximately 5 to 8 minutes, or until just tender. Toss the sautéed vegetables in with the potatoes, along with the dill weed and parsley. Mix together the cheese, sour cream or yogurt, and the milk. Pour this mixture in with the potatoes, then season with salt and pepper. Carefully mix and transfer to the prepared baking dish. Top with bread crumbs. Bake, uncovered, for approximately 30 minutes. Serves 8.

Nutrition information per serving, 8 servings per recipe: Calories: 291. Protein: 11g. Total fat: 8.9g (sat. fat: 5g). Carbohydrates: 40g. Cholesterol: 25mg. Sodium: 438mg. Vitamin A: 14% DV. Vitamin C: 66% DV.

DILL

This is not an exact recipe but more of a general guide on how to prepare simple and delicious oven-roasted potatoes. Adjust according to what vegetables and herbs you have on hand. Serve roasted vegetables with shish kabobs or veggie burgers, corn on the cob, thick tomato slices, a loaf of crusty French bread, and cold lemonade for a perfect summertime meal.

Roasted Potatoes with Fresh Herbs

Wash potatoes well, no need to peel (especially when they are organically grown!)—the skins are delicious and add color. Cut potatoes in large chunks and toss with enough olive oil to coat well. For variety, add large carrot chunks, peeled whole small beets, diced fresh garlic cloves, or thick onion slices. Season liberally with salt and freshly ground black pepper and place in a shallow baking dish or casserole. Bake uncovered in a 400°F oven until tender, approximately 35 to 45 minutes depending on the size of the vegetable chunks. Stir several times during baking, being careful not to break up potatoes. Fresh herbs such as rosemary, thyme, basil, or tarragon may be tossed in with the vegetables before baking. Chopped fresh parsley, chives, or dill weed may be tossed in right before serving. It's best to limit herbs to just one or two.

NUTRITION INFORMATION PER 2 TABLESPOONS DILL WEED, FRESH:

Calories: 2
Total fat: 0.6g
    (saturated fat: trace)
Fiber: <1g
Sodium: 3mg
Potassium: 1% Daily Value
Vitamin A: 7% Daily Value
Vitamin C: 6% Daily Value
Iron: 2% Daily Value
Calcium: 1% Daily Value

OREGANO

OREGANO

OREGANO derives its name from the Greek *oros,* meaning "mountain" and *ganos,* "joy". Far from its original roots in Europe, oregano flourishes in herb gardens almost everywhere, including our own in Kansas. This member of the mint family is a hardy and most prolific perennial, reaching a height of two feet. Later in the season, it will be covered with delicate pink flowers. Recorded culinary use of oregano dates back to the fourteenth century in Spain and Italy, with earlier use as a medicinal herb. Its popularity in the United States didn't really blossom until after World War II, but in the half century since, oregano has grown to become one of the most widely used dried herbs in this country.

HANDLING: If you have a sunny windowsill and a good-sized pot, or if you have a little corner of a yard or garden you can surrender, consider growing oregano. It is a very undemanding herb and will sprawl and grow without a lot of fussing. Then you will have an abundance of this "pizza herb". If you purchase fresh-cut oregano it will keep best tucked in a little jar with water in your refrigerator. If you have more than you know you can use, consider drying the surplus. Hang your little bunch of oregano upside down in a place where it will have good air flow but is out of direct sunlight. When it is totally dry and crumbly to the touch, strip the leaves from the stem and store in a tightly sealed container in a cool dark place. Although many cooks store their dried herbs and spices near the stovetop for convenience, you will compromise their flavor with the heat and light. Also, when you are cooking with dried herbs, avoid opening the jar and sprinkling the herbs directly into hot liquids. The heat and steam rising from the cooking pot can enter the jar and adversely affect the herb's quality—better to place the dried herbs in your hand to disperse into your dish.

SIMPLE PREPARATION: Besides its most popular use as a seasoning for pizza, oregano is at home in many other dishes. Little snips of the fresh herb are delicious in quiches, pasta sauces, and sautéed in olive oil and tossed with cooked pasta. Oregano tastes especially good in zucchini dishes, and in combination with garlic, parsley, and basil.

Peperonata is a slow-simmered stew of sweet peppers and onions. It can be a fairly simple affair or spiced up with herbs and garlic (as in this version). Not surprisingly, its roots are Italian. Serve peperonata with pieces of chewy Italian bread and hunks of fresh Parmesan cheese as an appetizer. Or use it as a topping for focaccia or pizza. It is also excellent mounded on top of homemade polenta.

Peperonata with Garlic and Fresh Oregano

2 tablespoons olive oil
4 to 6 garlic cloves, cut in slivers
1 medium-sized onion, cut in slivers
3 bell peppers, cut in slivers (most attractive if you have a variety of colors)
2 tablespoons water
2 tablespoons dry white wine
leaves from 1 sprig of fresh oregano
½ teaspoon salt
freshly ground black pepper to taste

Heat olive oil in a large, heavy skillet over medium heat. Add garlic, onions, and peppers. Sauté, stirring often, for approximately 5 minutes. Add remaining ingredients, reduce heat to medium-low. Simmer, covered, for approximately 20 to 25 minutes longer, or until vegetables are completely tender and almost creamy. Serve hot or at room temperature. Serves 4.

Nutrition information per serving, 4 servings per recipe: Calories: 91. Protein: 1g. Total fat: 6.4g (sat. fat: <1g). Carbohydrates: 6g. Cholesterol: 0mg. Sodium: 271mg. Vitamin A: 13% DV. Vitamin C: 143% DV.

Polenta is thick cornmeal mush with a romantic name and Italian credentials. It is inexpensive and simple to prepare although it does require your undivided attention for about fifteen minutes or you will spend at least that much time scouring out a scorched pot. Feel free to add grated Parmesan cheese, a dab of butter, or chopped fresh herbs right before serving.

Basic Polenta

1 cup coarsely ground cornmeal
1 cup cold water
1 teaspoon salt
3 cups boiling water

Combine cornmeal, cold water, and salt until thoroughly blended. In a saucepan bring 3 cups water to a full boil and, stirring constantly, gradually add cornmeal mixture (a wire whisk is helpful to avoid lumps). Cook, stirring continuously, over medium-low heat for 10 to 15 minutes or until the polenta is thick and smooth. You can stop right here and dish up the polenta hot and top with Peperonata and a sprinkle of cheese. *Or* you can go on and do something really fun, and traditional. You can clear off a large section of your kitchen countertop or table, wet it down with cold water, and spoon your hot polenta out of the pot and onto your prepared surface (kids love this part!). Smooth it all out to about ½ inch thick and let it sit there, lightly covered, to cool for at least an hour or longer. As you can imagine, the polenta will become firm. You can cut it in fun shapes, either with a knife or cookie cutters. Then brush the pieces of polenta with olive oil and bake it, grill it, or pan-fry it. One of our family's favorite ways to eat polenta is to grill pieces in olive oil then top with spaghetti sauce and grated smoked Provolone cheese. Basic recipe serves 6.

Nutrition information per serving, 6 servings per recipe: Calories: 73. Protein: 2g. Total fat: <1g (sat. fat: <1g). Carbohydrates: 15g. Cholesterol: 0mg. Sodium: 356mg. Vitamin A: 3% DV. Vitamin C: 0% DV.

If you have an abundance of fresh oregano, put some away in oil and/or vinegar either for yourself or to give away as handmade gifts. Flavored oils are wonderful in salad dressings or tossed with hot pasta. They will offer a reminder of summer on a rainy fall day.

Oil Infused with Fresh Oregano

2 cups canola or olive oil
1 cup chopped fresh oregano

Place oregano in a large glass jar (a quart canning jar will work well). Pour oil over oregano. Cover jar and let stand at room temperature for 4 to 5 days to allow oil to absorb flavor. Carefully pour or ladle oil off the herb into small clean jars. Discard oregano. Store oil, tightly capped, in refrigerator for up to 6 months.

Red Wine Vinegar with Fresh Oregano

Wash and dry a large bunch of very fresh oregano. Stuff into clean pint or quart jars. Fill jars with red wine vinegar. Cover and place on sunny windowsill for approximately one month. Pour steeped vinegar through cheesecloth or a paper filter. Discard oregano. Heat flavored vinegar to just a simmer and pour into hot sterilized jars. Cap or cork jars. Store in a cool dark place. Keeps for approximately 1 year.

NUTRITION INFORMATION PER 2 TABLESPOONS OREGANO, DRIED:

Calories: 30
Total fat: 0.7g
    (saturated fat: 0g)
Fiber: trace
Sodium: trace
Potassium: 4% Daily Value
Vitamin A: 6% Daily Value
Vitamin C: trace
Iron: 23% Daily Value
Calcium: 14% Daily Value

OREGANO

PARSLEY

PARSLEY is often assigned the lowly status of plate decoration. In reality, it is one of the most versatile and humble of all fresh herbs, as well as being a nutritional bargain. Its bright, clean taste is welcome raw; it also does well sautéed or slow cooked in soups, sauces, and stews. Parsley is a member of the carrot family and most of us will find this utilitarian herb readily available in one of two varieties; the more mild curly-leaf parsley, *Petroselinum crispum,* or flat-leaf Italian parsley, *Petroselinum neapolitanum.* Italian parsley has a fuller flavor and is more tender than curly leaf, but be careful not to accidentally grab a bunch of its lookalike cousin, cilantro. The two herbs are definitely not interchangeable.

HANDLING: Like any fresh herb, parsley will keep best stored like a bouquet in a glass of water in the refrigerator. The truth of the matter is, parsley also tolerates neglect and will survive for quite a few days stored loosely in a plastic bag or covered container in the fridge. You need to remove the tight-fitting band that usually binds the bunch together and cull out any damaged or yellow stems before you stow your parsley away. The key to keeping this hardy herb in good shape is to give it room so that the stems aren't bunched together tightly—once they start to decompose the whole bunch goes quickly.

SIMPLE PREPARATION: There's nothing like a big pile of finely chopped, bright green parsley to improve any recipe. Unlike some herbs that can easily ruin a dish if used in large quantities, parsley is almost never overpowering. Use in green salads and vinaigrette dressings, in bread stuffings, and toss into almost any cold marinated salad. Parsley is a natural companion to pasta, potato, and egg dishes. It is an essential ingredient in tabouli salad, and can be mixed with basil to create a lovely pesto. For a quick summer side dish, arrange thick slices of garden-fresh tomatoes on a platter, drizzle with olive oil and a splash of balsamic vinegar, and top with minced fresh parsley and basil, and some crumbles of Feta cheese.

Here is an impressive dish, special enough for company yet simple enough to be made in the time it takes to boil pasta. Cooked fettuccini is tossed with hot olive oil studded with dried tomatoes, garlic, and lots of fresh parsley. It doesn't get much finer.

Fettuccine with Parsley and Sun-dried Tomatoes

   1 pound fettuccini (uncooked)
   6 tablespoons olive oil
   6 garlic cloves, finely minced
   ½ cup sun-dried tomatoes, soaked in boiling water, drained, and cut in slivers
   ½ cup minced parsley
   ¾ teaspoon salt
   freshly ground black pepper
   freshly grated Parmesan cheese (optional)

Bring a large pot of water to a boil and cook the pasta while you prepare the sauce. Heat oil in a small skillet over medium heat. Add garlic and sauté for 3 to 5 minutes. Add tomato slivers to the olive oil and garlic. Continue to simmer for several minutes longer. Drain pasta. Return to cooking pot. Pour hot olive oil mixture over pasta. Add the parsley, salt, and plenty of black pepper. Toss until well combined. Serve immediately. Top with Parmesan. Serves 8.

Nutrition information per serving, 8 servings per recipe: Calories: 249. Protein: 5g. Total fat: 9.9g (sat. fat: 1.4g). Carbohydrates: 33g. Cholesterol: 0mg. Sodium: 208mg. Vitamin A: 4% DV. Vitamin C: 9% DV.

When the weather is hot, and tomatoes and cucumbers are plentiful (these times usually coincide), tabouli is in order. This refreshing and satisfying salad is quick to make and keeps well. Add a cup or two of cooked garbanzos to create a main dish. Serve with wedges of thick, chewy pita bread.

Tabouli

1¼ cups boiling water
1 cup uncooked bulgur wheat
3 green onions or 1 small regular onion, minced
1 to 2 tomatoes, chopped*
2 carrots, diced
1 cucumber, diced
3 tablespoons olive oil
3 tablespoons lemon juice
½ cup minced fresh parsley
1 to 2 teaspoons fresh mint, minced (or ¼ to ½ teaspoon dried mint)
1 to 2 cloves garlic, minced or pressed
¾ teaspoon salt
¼ teaspoon black pepper

Pour boiling water over bulgur in a large bowl. Cover, stir occasionally, and allow bulgur to absorb water (this will take about ½ hour). Uncover and allow bulgur to cool completely. Add remaining ingredients and toss thoroughly. Allow to marinate, refrigerated, for at least an hour before serving. Toss well again and adjust seasoning if necessary. Serves 5.

*If you intend to store your tabouli for several days' worth of feasting, it's best to put the tomatoes in as you serve it. Cut up tomatoes just don't keep well and, if mixed in, will shorten the life of the tabouli.

Nutrition information per serving, 5 servings per recipe: Calories: 219. Protein: 5g. Total fat: 7.9g (sat. fat: 1.1g). Carbohydrates: 31g. Cholesterol: 0mg. Sodium: 340mg. Vitamin A: 93% DV. Vitamin C: 44% DV.

The pale colors of fresh corn, white beans, and celery combine to create a delicate-looking salad, flecked with chopped parsley and slivers of dark red, dried tomatoes. Beneath its subtle appearance, however, lies the kick of a hot pepper. Perfect!

White Bean Salad with Fresh Corn

2 cups cooked navy beans, drained and rinsed
1 cup fresh corn, cut off the cob, lightly steamed
2 stalks celery, diced
1 shallot, minced
6 dried tomato halves, softened in boiling water, then cut into slivers
1 hot pepper, seeded and minced
¼ cup minced fresh parsley
3 tablespoons fresh lemon juice
2 tablespoons olive oil
½ teaspoon salt

Mix all ingredients together. Refrigerate for several hours before serving to allow flavors to blend. Serves 6.

Nutrition information per serving, 6 servings per recipe: Calories: 153. Protein: 5g. Total fat: 4.5g (sat. fat: <1g). Carbohydrates: 22g. Cholesterol: 0mg. Sodium: 178mg. Vitamin A: 3% DV. Vitamin C: 48% DV.

Parsley's fresh taste is at the center of this versatile green sauce. Not quite as thick as a pesto, this richly flavored sauce can be used as a topping for vegetables or as an embellishment for hot cream-based soups. Also good drizzled on hot pasta, as a dip for hunks of crusty Italian bread, or to dress up thick slices of fresh tomatoes.

The Very Freshest Green Dressing

1½ cups packed parsley leaves (the Italian variety will yield a better flavor)
2 garlic cloves, chopped
1 small shallot, chopped
juice of 1 lemon
6 tablespoons olive oil
1 tablespoon red wine vinegar
½ teaspoon salt
freshly ground black pepper

Combine all ingredients in a food processor and blend to create a smooth sauce. Allow to sit several hours before serving so that flavors have time to blend. Adjust seasonings if necessary. Although best used when fresh, this dressing will keep for 5 to 6 days covered in the refrigerator. Makes approximately 1½ cups.

Nutrition information per 2 tablespoons: Calories: 67. Protein: 0g. Total fat: 6.3g (sat. fat: <1g). Carbohydrates: 2g. Cholesterol: 0mg. Sodium: 92mg. Vitamin A: 4% DV. Vitamin C: 18% DV.

NUTRITION INFORMATION PER 2 TABLESPOONS PARSLEY, FRESH:

Calories: 3
Total fat: 0g
   (saturated fat: 0g)
Fiber: 0.3g
Sodium: 3mg
Potassium: 1% Daily Value
Vitamin A: 4% Daily Value
Vitamin C: 11% Daily Value
Iron: 3% Daily Value
Calcium: 1% Daily Value

ROSEMARY

ROSEMARY was once part of the official pharmacopoeia of Rome. It is an herb with much symbolism, folklore, medicinal, historical, and, of course, culinary history attached to it. Its name is derived from the Latin, *ros marinus,* dew of the sea. Rosemary's romantic name is appropriate to its roots as an evergreen shrub, native to the Mediterranean, flourishing when grown by the sea. In fact, its leaves look more like pine needles than true leaves and its taste hints of fir and balsam. Beautiful enough to be used as decorative foliage, rosemary is not one of the more popular herbs in this country, but is highly favored in parts of Italy where a fresh rosemary sprig is included with purchases from the butcher shop.

HANDLING: Store rosemary in a plastic bag in your refrigerator. Or make a little bundle of it to hang in the kitchen to dry. Since rosemary leaves do not soften much in cooking, a good way to enjoy its flavor is to place fresh rosemary in a bottle of olive oil and allow its flavor to infuse the oil.

SIMPLE PREPARATION: If you'll be using rosemary fresh it is best to mince it finely. You can also use the whole sprig when cooking liquids such as soup or broth and remove the sprig before serving. Another way to release the flavor of rosemary is to heat olive oil or butter and allow the sprig to simmer in the oil or butter for a few minutes, then remove the rosemary and proceed with your recipe. There's nothing wrong with eating the leaves of rosemary, it's just that they remain somewhat dense even when cooked. Rosemary is most wonderful in combination with potatoes and delicious with green beans too!

If you've hesitated making focaccia because it seems complicated, or because you fear dealing with yeast, give this recipe a try. Hot, homemade focaccia is like nothing you can buy anywhere. You will need some time to make it—not that it requires a lot of tending, but because you must allow time for the yeast to do what it does best—bring bread to life!

Rosemary Focaccia with Onions and Garlic

3 to 4 tablespoons olive oil
1 medium-sized onion, coarsely chopped
2 to 4 cloves garlic, finely minced
1 cup warm water (between 105°F and 115°F)
1 teaspoon sugar or honey
1 tablespoon active dry yeast
3 cups flour (unbleached white, or white mixed with no more than 1 cup whole wheat)
1 teaspoon salt
2 tablespoons finely minced rosemary
extra flour for kneading
1 tablespoon cornmeal

Heat 1 tablespoon of the oil in a small skillet over medium-low heat. Add onions and garlic to pan and sauté slowly until completely tender and golden. Set aside. Place warm water in a small bowl. Dissolve the sweetener in the water, then sprinkle the yeast on top. Stir to mix well. Allow yeast mixture to sit for several minutes until yeast begins to bubble to surface. Transfer this mixture to a larger bowl, add one tablespoon of oil, the sautéed onions and garlic, and half of the flour. Beat mixture with a wooden spoon for two minutes. Add salt and 1 tablespoon of the rosemary. Add flour ½ cup at a time until the dough comes together. It should be soft but not too sticky. Turn the dough out onto a floured surface and knead for several minutes, adding extra flour as needed to keep dough from sticking to your hands and the surface you're working on. The dough should be fairly smooth and elastic. Form the dough into a ball and place in a medium-sized, oiled bowl. Cover with a light towel and allow dough to rise in a warm, draft-free place for approximately 45 minutes or until doubled in size. Punch dough down, and once again, dump out onto a floured surface. Knead very lightly, then using your fingers or a rolling pin, begin working the dough out into a flat rectangular shape. Allow to rest a few minutes while you oil a large, flat baking sheet with olive oil. Dust the sheet with cornmeal. Carefully lift the focaccia onto the sheet, and use your fingers to press the dough out to its final size, approximately 10 x 14 inches. Cover with a towel and allow to rise again, this time for about 30 minutes. Toward the end of the rising, preheat the oven to 400°F. Before placing the focaccia in the oven, use your fingers to press a number of indentations in the top. Brush with the remaining olive oil and sprinkle with the remaining tablespoon of chopped fresh rosemary (and grated Parmesan for a real treat!). Bake for approximately 20 minutes. The focaccia should be golden brown and hollow sounding when lightly tapped. Serve hot! Makes 9 large pieces.

Nutrition information per piece, 9 pieces per recipe: Calories: 187. Protein: 5g. Total fat: 4.6g (sat. fat: <1g). Carbohydrates: 31g. Cholesterol: 0mg. Sodium: 238mg. Vitamin A: <1% DV. Vitamin C: 3% DV.

Potatoes, green beans, and rosemary are quite a compatible trio—especially delicious together when the potatoes and beans are garden-fresh!

Potatoes and Green Beans with Fresh Rosemary

1 pound small new potatoes
1 pound fresh green beans
2 tablespoons fresh lemon juice
2 tablespoons olive oil
1 to 2 sprigs fresh rosemary, finely minced
1 garlic clove, finely minced
½ teaspoon salt
black pepper to taste

Wash but don't peel potatoes. If they are small, leave them whole. Cut larger potatoes in half. Boil or steam until just tender. While potatoes are cooking prepare the beans. Cut or snap beans in half and very lightly steam. When potatoes and beans are done, arrange them on a platter. Mix together remaining ingredients. Drizzle this dressing over potatoes and beans. Embellish plate with additional sprigs of rosemary. Serve warm. Serves 6.

Nutrition information per serving, 6 servings per recipe: Calories: 135. Protein: 2g. Total fat: 4.4g (sat. fat: <1g). Carbohydrates: 21g. Cholesterol: 0mg. Sodium: 184mg. Vitamin A: 5% DV. Vitamin C: 33% DV.

NUTRITION INFORMATION PER 2 TABLESPOONS ROSEMARY, DRIED:

Calories: 24
Total fat: 0g
   (saturated fat: 0g)
Fiber: trace
Sodium: 6mg
Potassium: 2% Daily Value
Vitamin A: 2% Daily Value
Vitamin C: 10% Daily Value
Iron: 13% Daily Value
Calcium: 9% Daily Value

Vegetables

ASPARAGUS

ASPARAGUS

ASPARAGUS has been around as long as the Great Pyramids. Ancient Egyptians enjoyed the wild variety, and the Romans learned to cultivate it. There are three main types of asparagus: green, white, and purple. One attribute of asparagus that you may have noticed is its effect as a kidney diuretic, breaking up oxalic acid and uric acid crystals in the kidneys and muscles and eliminating them through the urine. This is why we sometimes notice a strong smell in our urine after consuming asparagus. Don't be concerned; this is actually a good thing —and a temporary condition.

HANDLING: Asparagus needs to be treated quite carefully to retain its fresh flavor. Trim off the very ends of the spears and place them upright in an inch of water in your refrigerator. Before cooking, decide whether or not to peel your asparagus. If the asparagus is young and small, there's no need to peel. Just snap off the tougher ends and you're ready to go. Peeling bigger or older stalks makes them more edible.

SIMPLE PREPARATION: The easiest way to prepare asparagus is to blanch or boil whole spears or pieces. Bring a pan of water (three-fourths full) to a boil. Ideally, your pan would be large enough to allow whole spears to lie flat. You may choose to salt your water. Place the asparagus into the boiling water and bring to a full boil again. Cook for approximately 4 minutes and then start testing for doneness. Cooked asparagus should be slightly tender when pierced with a fork but still beautifully green and fresh tasting. Steaming also works well. If you're going to use asparagus for a cold dish, rinse in cold water and drain completely.

Pieces of sweet roasted onion, tender potatoes, and almost crisp asparagus perfectly complement the pasta in this delicious main dish— impressive to serve company. Just add a green salad and a loaf of chewy Italian bread for a feast.

Penne with Potatoes and Asparagus

2 tablespoons olive oil
1 large onion, coarsely chopped (2 to 2½ cups)
1 pound small waxy potatoes, cut in thick slices, then cut in half (4 cups)
1 teaspoon salt
several sprigs fresh thyme (optional)
½ pound penne pasta
1 pound asparagus, cut into 1 to 2-inch pieces
several splashes balsamic vinegar
freshly ground black pepper to taste
¼ cup fresh basil leaves, cut into thin ribbons
freshly grated Parmesan cheese

Preheat oven to 375°F. Put on a large pot of water to cook the pasta. Pour oil in a 9 x 13-inch baking pan. Put the onions and potatoes in the pan, sprinkle with ½ teaspoon salt, add the sprigs of thyme, and mix well to coat vegetables with oil. Bake, uncovered, for approximately 15 minutes (vegetables should be almost tender). While vegetables are roasting, cook the pasta until just tender, drain, and set aside (the timing should be such that your pasta will be cooked about the time you'll be adding it to the dish). Remove vegetables from the oven. Add the asparagus and the cooked pasta. Season with remaining ½ teaspoon salt, several splashes balsamic vinegar, black pepper, and the fresh basil. Toss carefully until vegetables and pasta are evenly mixed. Return to oven, uncovered, for 10 minutes. Bring steaming to the table with a bowl of Parmesan cheese to sprinkle on top. Serves 6.

Nutrition information per serving, 6 servings per recipe: Calories: 205. Protein: 5g. Total fat: 4.7g (sat. fat: <1g). Carbohydrates: 36. Cholesterol: 0mg. Sodium: 367mg. Vitamin A: 6% DV. Vitamin C: 51% DV.

Choosing just the right shape of pasta for a recipe is a fun process, and can change the personality of your recipe. Be creative with this dependable and delicious salad.

Marinated Pasta and Asparagus Salad

1 pound pasta (penne, bowties, spirals or other shape of your choosing)
2 cups sliced asparagus
½ cup green onions, sliced diagonally
1 green or red pepper, cut in slivers
⅓ cup chopped black olives (optional)
6 tablespoons olive oil*
4 tablespoons herb vinegar or balsamic vinegar*
1 teaspoon each dried basil and oregano (or 2 tablespoons fresh herbs)
½ teaspoon salt
several generous grinds of black pepper

Boil pasta until cooked but still firm. Rinse under cool running water, drain well, and set aside. Cook asparagus until just tender-crisp and still bright green. Rinse under cool running water, set aside. Mix asparagus, green onions, green or red pepper, and black olives with cooled pasta and toss lightly with oil, vinegar, and herbs. Season with salt and pepper. Cover and chill thoroughly. Serves 8.

*10 tablespoons low-fat Italian dressing can be substituted for the oil and vinegar.

Nutrition information per serving, 8 servings per recipe: Calories: 183. Protein: 3g. Total fat: 11.7g (sat. fat: 1.8g). Carbohydrates: 16g. Cholesterol: 0mg. Sodium: 211mg. Vitamin A: 7% DV. Vitamin C: 40% DV.

Risotto is a creamy rice dish made from very glutinous short-grained Arborio rice. Arborio rice takes some tending during cooking but the results are worth the effort.

Creamy Asparagus Risotto

½ pound asparagus
2½ to 3 cups vegetable stock
1½ tablespoons olive oil
2 shallots, minced
¼ cup dry white wine or stock
1 cup Arborio rice
⅓ cup freshly grated Parmesan or Asiago cheese
2 tablespoons chopped fresh parsley

Cut tips from the asparagus. Cut stems into ½ inch pieces. Set aside. Heat stock to boiling, reduce heat to simmer, and hold there until ready to use. Sauté shallots in olive oil in a large, heavy skillet or saucepan over medium heat until softened, approximately 5 minutes. Add the asparagus stems and the wine. Cook, stirring frequently, until most of the wine has evaporated and the asparagus is somewhat tender. Carefully add the rice to the skillet, stirring gently until well mixed. Add 1 cup of the simmering stock. Cook, uncovered, over medium-low heat until liquid is absorbed, approximately 10 minutes. Do not stir. Pour 1 more cup of the simmering stock into the rice and allow to cook until liquid is absorbed, approximately 10 more minutes. Carefully stir in the asparagus tips and the remaining stock. Cook until all liquid is absorbed. At this point the rice should be tender. If necessary add additional stock and simmer until rice is fully cooked. Remove from heat. Stir in cheese and parsley. Serve immediately. Serves 4.

Nutrition information per serving, 4 servings per recipe: Calories: 214. Protein: 7g. Total fat: 8g (sat. fat: 2.2g). Carbohydrates: 27g. Cholesterol: 6.5mg. Sodium: 241mg. Vitamin A: 26% DV. Vitamin C: 29% DV.

NUTRITION INFORMATION PER 4 SPEARS ASPARAGUS, COOKED:

Calories: 15
Total fat: <0.2g
      (saturated fat: <0.2g)
Fiber: 1g
Sodium: 3mg
Potassium: 5% Daily Value
Vitamin A: 5% Daily Value
Vitamin C: 27% Daily Value
Iron: 2% Daily Value
Calcium: 2% Daily Value

BEETS come to our tables in many forms. Brownish-white, fibrous sugar beets feed our passion for sweets in the form of white sugar. Beet greens and Swiss chard (a lcaf beet) provide us with nutrient-dense foliage for cooking. The deep crimson and golden round roots are what we usually think of when we hear the word "beet" or *Beta vulgaris,* named for its resemblance to the second letter of the Greek alphabet. In Europe, huge mangels or mangold beets are grown mostly as animal fodder, sometimes weighing as much as 60 pounds—quite a feast for a cow!

HANDLING: If your beets come with the greens attached, so much the better—you have two vegetables. Before storing in the refrigerator cut the greens off the root, leaving approximately two inches of greens attached to the crown to prevent bleeding. For the same reason leave the root stem in place. For longer storage life do not wash your beets before you refrigerate them, as wet beets tend to rot. Store your greens in a roomy, unsealed plastic bag. Try to make use of your fresh greens right away—they are perishable and not nearly as patient as the roots.

SIMPLE PREPARATION: Beets are delicious and gorgeous when eaten raw. Peel and coarsely grate as an addition to salads or to add crunch and variety to sandwiches. A small amount of raw grated beets will turn your slaw a beautiful rose color. If you prefer to cook your beets, trim greens down to within an inch of the root. Scrub your beets but don't peel them—you'll need those skins to help hold in the color. Baking and steaming are both good ways to prepare beets. To bake, place whole beets in a casserole dish, add a small amount of water, cover, and cook in a 350°F oven until beets are fork-tender and skins easily slip off. This will take between 45 minutes and an hour, depending on the size of the beets. If your beets are particularly large you may want to peel and quarter them, drizzle with olive oil, sprinkle with salt and pepper, cover, and bake until fork-tender. Steaming is a simple way to prepare beets, especially if you'll be using them in a cold salad. Place whole, unpeeled beets in the steamer basket and cook until fork-tender (approximately 40 minutes for a 1½- inch-diameter beet, or under pressure about 10 minutes). Place cooked beets briefly under cold running water—the skins should slip right off.

Here is a visually striking combination—the red beets enhance the green peel of the apples to create a glorious and delicious salad. Inspiration for this recipe comes from Renee Shepherd and Fran Raboff, authors of *More Recipe from a Kitchen Garden*.

Gorgeous Beet and Apple Salad

4 to 5 medium-sized beets, cooked, cut into large cubes
1 large Granny Smith apple, unpeeled, cut into large cubes
1/4 cup slivered red onion
1 tablespoon canola oil
1 teaspoon balsamic vinegar (or red wine vinegar)
1/4 teaspoon salt
1 teaspoon Dijon mustard
1 tablespoon minced shallots
1/4 teaspoon sugar or honey

Toss beets, apples, and red onions together in a medium-sized bowl. Mix remaining ingredients to create the dressing. Pour over vegetables and toss to mix well. Chill. Serves 4.

Nutrition information per serving, 4 servings per recipe: Calories: 86. Protein: <1g. Total fat: 3.6g (sat. fat: <1g). Carbohydrates:12 g. Cholesterol: 0mg. Sodium: 197mg. Vitamin A: <1% DV. Vitamin C: 13% DV.

Quick Grated Beets are beautiful, tasty, and easy...what more could you ask for?

Quick Grated Beets

4 medium-sized beets
1 tablespoon butter or olive oil
1 to 3 tablespoons fresh lemon juice (to taste)
3 to 6 tablespoons water or vegetable stock
1/2 teaspoon salt
freshly ground black pepper to taste
chopped fresh dill or parsley

Wash, peel, and coarsely grate beets. Heat butter or oil in a medium-sized skillet over medium-low heat. Add beets, and stir to coat well. Sprinkle with lemon juice, cover, and cook for approximately 10 minutes. Stir occasionally and add water or stock as needed to prevent scorching. Cook until just tender. Season with salt and pepper. Sprinkle with dill or parsley. Serve immediately. Serves 4.

Nutrition information per serving, 4 servings per recipe: Calories: 48. Protein: <1g. Total fat: 3.2g (sat. fat: <1g). Carbohydrates: 4g. Cholesterol: 0mg. Sodium: 267mg. Vitamin A: 0% DV. Vitamin C: 11% DV.

Potatoes and beets pair up in this slightly different home fry recipe. It's a great combination, accented with red bell pepper and the fresh taste of parsley.

Rosy Home Fries

4 to 5 medium potatoes, cooked until tender but still firm, then cubed
3 medium beets, cooked until tender, peeled, and cubed
1 tablespoon canola oil
1 medium onion, finely chopped
1 large red pepper, chopped
½ cup minced fresh parsley
¾ teaspoon salt
black pepper to taste

Heat the oil in a large skillet over medium heat. Add the onions and sauté for 5 minutes, stirring often. Add the potatoes and beets and sauté for approximately 10 more minutes, stirring occasionally, until the potatoes begin to brown slightly. Remove from heat. Toss in the red pepper, parsley, salt, and pepper. Serve immediately. Serves 6.

Nutrition information per serving, 6 servings per recipe: Calories: 118. Protein: 2 g. Total fat: 2.2g (sat. fat: <1g). Carbohydrates: 22 g. Cholesterol: 0mg. Sodium: 267mg. Vitamin A: 10% DV. Vitamin C: 72% DV.

NUTRITION INFORMATION PER 2 BEETS, COOKED:

Calories: 31
Total fat: 0g
   (saturated fat: 0g)
Fiber: 2.5g
Sodium: 49mg
Potassium: 9% Daily Value
Vitamin A: <1% Daily Value
Vitamin C: 10% Daily Value
Iron: 3% Daily Value
Calcium: 1% Daily Value

BEETS

BOK CHOY

BOK CHOY, also known as Pak Choi, Baak Choi, and Taisai, is a member of the Brassicaceae or mustard family and is thereby a cousin to cabbages, radishes, turnips, mustards, and a number of other vegetable powerhouses. Bok choy is actually a variety of Chinese cabbage, but unlike the thick, full, pale heads of typical cabbages, bok choy has delicate greenish-white stalks that are topped with broad, dark leaves. Enjoy bok choy in stir-fry and try its sweet, delicate stalks raw as an alternative to celery.

HANDLING: Unwashed bok choy should be stored loosely in a plastic bag in your refrigerator. Bok choy isn't quite as durable as head cabbage; the dark leaves begin to wilt after several days.

SIMPLE PREPARATION: Tear the stalks away from the base and wash carefully. You'll want to separate the leafy greens from the stalks because they cook quite differently. Cut the leaves in ribbons, or chop coarsely for use in stir-fry. These will be added in the very last moments of cooking since they only require a minute or two to wilt. If you're using the stalks in stir-fry, slice them the same way you would slice celery—they are particularly attractive sliced on the diagonal and should be added several minutes before the greens. Bok choy stalks, especially when they are fresh and young, are wonderful eaten raw—as dippers or in salads.

Stir-frying involves quick-cooking foods while stirring them in a small amount of oil over high heat. This can be done in a wok or large frying pan. Vegetables retain their crispness and bright flavor. Have all ingredients ready before you begin cooking. Cut vegetables into uniform shapes and sizes. Before you begin stir-frying, take a look around you and enjoy the sight of all those fresh, beautiful vegetables lying ready in little piles on your counter.

Simple Stir-fry with Marinated Tofu

Marinade for tofu:
2 tablespoons canola oil
3 tablespoons reduced-sodium soy sauce
1 clove garlic, minced or pressed
½ tablespoon freshly grated ginger root
1 teaspoon honey or sugar

1 pound firm tofu
1 to 2 tablespoons canola oil to fry tofu
1 to 2 tablespoons peanut or sesame oil for stir-frying vegetables

Stir-fry vegetables: approximately 8 cups, any combination of prepared vegetables:
bok choy, stems cut on the diagonal, leaves cut into ribbons

onions, cut into crescents	carrots, cut into matchsticks
cauliflower, cut into thin slices	broccoli, cut into florets
fresh mushrooms, sliced	green peppers, cut into slivers
green onions, sliced diagonally	snap peas, whole or sliced on the diagonal

Prepare marinade by mixing the five marinade ingredients together in a medium-sized bowl. Prepare tofu by draining and patting dry with a towel. Cut tofu into long, thin strips approximately ¼-inch thick, 2 to 3-inches long. Heat canola oil in a large heavy skillet or wok over medium-high heat. Add tofu strips and cook, stirring often, until they're a little shriveled and lightly golden (approximately 10 minutes). The strips will slightly break down while they cook—this is okay. Drain the strips on a paper towel and toss them in the marinade. Set aside while you stir-fry the vegetables. Heat the peanut or sesame oil in the skillet or wok. If you are using onions, start your stir-fry with them. Stirring the whole time, add the firmest vegetables first (such as carrots, cauliflower), then medium-firm veggies (such as bok choy stems), and lastly, the most tender vegetables (such as the bok choy greens). When vegetables are just about tender-crisp, add the tofu and its marinade. Allow all to simmer until vegetables are cooked to perfection. Serve immediately over rice or noodles. Serves 4 very generously.

Nutrition information per serving, 4 servings per recipe, based on using a combination of vegetables and 4 tablespoons of oil: Calories: 274. Protein: 5g. Total fat: 17g (sat. fat: 2g). Carbohydrates: 25g. Cholesterol: 0mg. Sodium: 511mg. Vitamin A: 137% DV. Vitamin C: 153% DV.

Here is a quick stir-fry, delicious as a side dish to accompany pan-fried tofu and basmati rice. The apples are a nice complement to the bok choy. If you prefer a more savory taste, try the variation made with shiitake mushrooms.

Bok Choy with Apples

1½ pounds bok choy
1 tablespoon peanut oil
¼ cup onions, cut in slivers
1 teaspoon freshly grated ginger
1 tart green apple, cut in cubes
2 to 3 tablespoons vegetable broth or water
½ teaspoon salt

Cut leaves off the bok choy stems. Slice stems on the diagonal. Cut greens into ribbons. Set aside. Heat oil in a large skillet or wok over medium-high heat. Add onions and stir-fry for 1 to 2 minutes. Add ginger, then bok choy stems and apples. Stir in as much broth or water as needed to prevent scorching. Stir-fry for approximately 5 minutes. Add bok choy greens, sprinkle with salt, and stir-fry until just wilted. Serve immediately. Serves 4.

Variation: Bok Choy with Shiitake Mushrooms

Omit apples. Add 1 cup fresh shiitake mushrooms, cut in slivers. Substitute 1 teaspoon soy sauce for salt and add freshly ground black pepper to taste.

Nutrition information per serving, 4 servings per recipe: Calories: 78. Protein: 1g. Total fat: 3.2g (sat. fat: <1g). Carbohydrates: 9 g. Cholesterol: 0mg. Sodium: 379mg. Vitamin A: 51% DV. Vitamin C: 135% DV.

NUTRITION INFORMATION PER ½ CUP BOK CHOY, COOKED:

Calories: 10
Total fat: <0.2g
   (saturated fat: 0g)
Fiber: 1.3g
Sodium: 29mg
Potassium: 9% Daily Value
Vitamin A: 22% Daily Value
Vitamin C: 37% Daily Value
Iron: 5% Daily Value
Calcium: 8% Daily Value

BOK CHOY

BROCCOLI

BROCCOLI

BROCCOLI made a landmark trip across the United States in the 1920s after Italian market gardeners shipped crates of *Brassica oleracea italica* to Boston, and that was the beginning of its popularity. And why wouldn't it be popular? Broccoli is one of those seemingly flawless vegetables: usually affordable, extremely nutritious, patient in the refrigerator, almost always available, and so tasty when just lightly steamed. In more recent years we've heard a lot about phytochemicals and the possible role they may play as cancer fighters. Cruciferous vegetables, such as broccoli, contain heaps of these compounds, as well as beta-carotene, fiber, and a host of other nutrients. A definite must-eat on your vegetable list.

HANDLING: Fresh broccoli should be a deep color—almost bluish-green, with no yellow tinge. Store it in the refrigerator in a loose-fitting plastic bag. Broccoli does need to be washed carefully—it is sometimes home to aphids or well-camouflaged green cabbage worms. Fill your sink with cool water and immerse the whole head. The stalks can be scrubbed, but it is the green heads that will need the most attention as this is where the little critters will be living. After the initial rinsing, cut your broccoli heads from the stalk (don't throw those stalks away!) and begin separating the head into little florets, either with a knife or by breaking them apart. You can then rinse the florets under cool running water to further clean them. Broccoli stalks, as long as they aren't woody or too big, can be sliced thin and steamed with the florets. If the outer covering is rough or tough, it can be peeled to reveal the more tender inside stalk.

SIMPLE PREPARATION: Small broccoli florets and thin slices of stalk can be enjoyed raw in salads or as a part of a vegetable plate. However, a very, very light steaming or quick blanching softens the flavor and actually brings out a vivid green color, yet still leaves the broccoli crisp and virtually raw. Longer steaming or blanching is the easiest way to serve broccoli as a cooked vegetable, but take great care not to overcook! Cooked broccoli should always be a bright green and tender-crisp, never limp and greyish-green. Embellish lightly-cooked broccoli with a squeeze of lemon, drizzle of olive oil, a splash of balsamic vinegar, or a sprinkle of Parmesan cheese.

With just a little bit of work, steamed broccoli takes on a new look.

Broccoli with Herbed Crumb Topping

2 large stalks broccoli, steamed
1 tablespoon butter
1 cup breadcrumbs
¼ teaspoon dried savory
¼ teaspoon dried basil
½ teaspoon salt
freshly ground black pepper to taste
¼ cup chopped fresh parsley
¼ cup grated Parmesan cheese

To prepare broccoli for steaming, cut the crowns into little florets, and the stems into thin slices. Steam until tender-crisp. While the broccoli is steaming, prepare the crumb topping. Melt butter in a small heavy skillet over medium heat. Add bread crumbs, savory, and basil. Toast, stirring frequently, for 7 to 10 minutes. Remove from heat. Sprinkle salt, pepper, and parsley over bread crumbs and toss well. Add Parmesan and toss again. Place hot steamed broccoli in an attractive serving dish and sprinkle with herbed bread crumbs. Serves 6.

Nutrition information per serving, 6 servings per recipe: Calories: 115. Protein: 5g. Total fat: 3.7g (sat. fat: 2g). Carbohydrates: 15 g. Cholesterol: 9mg. Sodium: 400mg. Vitamin A: 13% DV. Vitamin C: 95% DV.

This scrumptious salad makes a perfect main course for a summertime lunch or potluck meal, accompanied by thick slices of dark bread and perfectly ripe melon wedges.

Cold Ravioli Salad with Dijon Vinaigrette

16 to 18 oz. frozen cheese-stuffed ravioli or tortelloni
½ cup red onion, sliced
½ cup fresh parsley, chopped
2 cups broccoli florets, lightly steamed
1 cup slivered carrots

Dressing:
3 to 4 tablespoons olive oil
2 tablespoons balsamic vinegar
1 tablespoon Dijon mustard
2 to 3 cloves garlic, pressed or minced
½ teaspoon salt
several generous grinds of black pepper

Cook pasta according to package directions and rinse under cold running water. Toss pasta carefully with vegetables. Mix dressing ingredients together and whisk or shake until well blended. Pour over pasta and vegetables, and toss carefully to evenly distribute dressing. Chill thoroughly. Serves 6 to 8.

Nutrition information per serving, 6 servings per recipe: Calories: 331. Protein: 13g. Total fat: 18.1g (sat. fat: 8.1g). Carbohydrates: 28g. Cholesterol: 86mg. Sodium: 643mg. Vitamin A: 65% DV. Vitamin C: 59% DV.

This is simple fare, but very satisfying. Tofu is especially good added to this dish.. Cut firm tofu into ½-inch cubes and add to the skillet when you sauté the garlic and broccoli.

Very Simple Pasta and Broccoli

    1 pound pasta (penne, ziti, or bowties)
    1 large bunch broccoli
    2 tablespoons olive oil
    4 to 6 cloves garlic, finely minced
    lots of freshly ground black pepper
    1 tablespoon reduced-sodium soy sauce
    freshly grated Parmesan cheese

Cook pasta until done but still firm. While it is cooking, prepare the broccoli. Cut stems and flowers into bite-size pieces. Heat oil in a large skillet over medium heat. Add garlic and broccoli. Sauté until garlic is golden and broccoli is tender-crisp. If broccoli begins to stick, add several tablespoons of water, broth, or white wine to help steam. Season with soy sauce and black pepper. Serve immediately over hot cooked pasta and pass around the grated cheese. Serves 4 to 6.

Nutrition information per serving, 4 servings per recipe: Calories: 217. Protein: 6g. Total fat: 6.9g (sat. fat: <1g). Carbohydrates: 32g. Cholesterol: 0mg. Sodium: 176mg. Vitamin A: 14% DV. Vitamin C: 139% DV.

NUTRITION INFORMATION PER ½ CUP BROCCOLI, COOKED:

Calories: 23
Total fat: <0.2g
    (saturated fat: 0g)
Fiber: 2.1g
Sodium: 8mg
Potassium: 4% Daily Value
Vitamin A: 11% Daily Value
Vitamin C: 82% Daily Value
Iron: 5% Daily Value
Calcium: 9% Daily Value

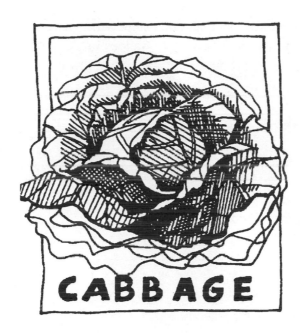

CABBAGE

CABBAGE has long been a staple in American cuisine. Thomas Jefferson purportedly grew 22 different varieties of cabbage in his Monticello garden. W. Atlee Burpee offered the Surehead cabbage seed to gardeners in 1877. And anyone who's eaten at a traditional New England restaurant has surely seen some variation of the New England Boiled Dinner described on the menu. Cole slaw, sauerkraut, cabbage rolls, cabbage soup, even cabbage strudel—solid, dependable cabbage in its many forms. Besides the more standard tight green heads, enjoy the different flavor and texture of crinkly Savoy cabbage or the deep, rich color of red cabbage.

HANDLING: Cabbage is an excellent keeper, especially the firm, compact varieties. It will store for at least 2 weeks in your refrigerator. The looser varieties will keep for about a week. At temperatures of 32°F with high humidity, cabbage will keep for months, but it will smell stronger over time.

SIMPLE PREPARATION: Remove tough or damaged outer leaves and rinse off any dirt. Trim the stem end. Halve or quarter cabbage along the core to make it easier to work with. To steam, cut 2 to 3-inch wedges off the core and place in a steamer. Steam for approximately 10 minutes, just long enough so that it can be pierced with a fork. Be careful to not overcook cabbage—the texture will become mushy and the flavor will be strong. Steam sliced carrots along with your cabbage for a tasty, simple side dish. Head cabbage is easily chopped or grated to add to salad or slaw, and red cabbage is an especially nice color addition. Savoy and other loose-leaf cabbages have thinner leaves and cook more quickly.

This is a very adaptable recipe. You can make this stew with whatever vegetables you have on hand. It is delicious made with potatoes or sweet potatoes in place of the turnips. Serve on top of a generous scoop of brown rice. At our house we almost always serve this cozy stew with hot homemade biscuits.

Tofu Vegetable Stew

2 tablespoons canola oil
1 large onion, chopped
2 cloves garlic, minced or pressed
1 pound firm tofu, cut into ½-inch cubes
2 medium carrots, sliced
¼ to ½ head of cabbage, chopped
1 cup turnip or rutabaga, chopped
3 to 4 cups stock or water
5 tablespoons reduced-sodium soy sauce
1 bay leaf

Heat oil in a soup pot over medium heat. Sauté onions and garlic for 2 to 3 minutes. Add tofu cubes and sauté several more minutes. Add remaining ingredients. Bring to a boil, reduce heat to medium low and simmer, covered, for 35 to 45 minutes. Serves 6.

Nutrition information per serving, 6 servings per recipe: Calories: 261. Protein: 13g. Total fat: 6.9g (sat. fat: <1g). Carbohydrates: 37g. Cholesterol: 0mg. Sodium: 520mg. Vitamin A: 86% DV. Vitamin C: 27% DV.

This homey and satisfying soup is a reliable family favorite.

Cabbage Potato Soup

1 medium onion
1 small cabbage, shredded
¾ teaspoon salt
¼ to ½ teaspoon black pepper
4 potatoes, diced
4 carrots, diced
1 cup light sour cream
1 teaspoon dried dill weed

In a large soup pot cook onion, cabbage, salt, and pepper together in enough water to cover, until just tender. In another pot, cook potatoes and carrots in enough water to cover. When potatoes are tender, drain potato water into pot with cabbage and onions. Mash potato-carrot mixture together with sour cream and dill weed. Add sour cream mixture to cabbage broth very slowly, to avoid curdling. Stir continually during this part. Adjust seasoning if necessary and serve immediately. Serves 6.

Nutrition information per serving, 6 servings per recipe: Calories: 190. Protein: 3g. Total fat: 6.8g (sat. fat: 4.1g). Carbohydrates: 29g. Cholesterol: 13mg. Sodium: 356mg. Vitamin A: 182% DV. Vitamin C: 55% DV.

Here is an almost-classic cole slaw enhanced by the added sweetness of apples and raisins.

Slaw with Apples and Raisins

4 cups coarsely chopped or grated cabbage
2 to 3 medium-sized carrots, coarsely grated
1 tart apple, finely diced
½ cup raisins
⅓ cup light salad dressing*
½ teaspoon salt

Toss all ingredients together until dressing is evenly distributed. Chill before serving. Serves 6.

*Use your favorite reduced-fat mayonnaise or salad dressing. I use a product called Nayonaise® that is made from tofu rather than eggs and oil. I like its light taste and its nutritional profile—no cholesterol and just 3 grams of fat per serving. There is also a fat-free Nayonaise®, although I must say I like the taste of the original version better.

Nutrition information per serving, 6 servings per recipe: Calories 100. Protein: 1g. Total fat: 2.6g (sat. fat: <1g). Carbohydrates: 17g. Cholesterol: 0mg. Sodium: 283mg. Vitamin A: 68% DV. Vitamin C: 45% DV.

NUTRITION INFORMATION PER ½ CUP CABBAGE, RAW:

Calories: 16
Total fat: <0.2g
    (saturated fat: 0g)
Fiber: 1.6g
Sodium: 14mg
Potassium: 4% Daily Value
Vitamin A: <1% Daily Value
Vitamin C: 30% Daily Value
Iron: 2% Daily Value
Calcium: 3% Daily Value

CABBAGE

CARROTS

CARROTS weren't always orange. Their ancestors were probably purple, spindly, and not very tasty. We can thank the Dutch for developing the orange carrot in the seventeenth century. Many refinements have followed to create sweeter, shorter, longer, better storing, more uniform roots (and that's what carrots are—roots). We must like the results since the annual American per capita consumption of carrots is 10 pounds, making it one of the more popular veggies. If an apple a day is good advice, then a carrot a day would be supreme advice, since one humble carrot contains 203 percent of your daily need for vitamin A. If you eat enough carrots your skin will develop a subtle orange hue, especially noticeable on the palms of your hands. Officially known as carotenemia, this is a harmless and temporary condition.

HANDLING: Carrots should be solid and firm. If your carrots come with fresh lacy "tops" that are crisp and green, this is an indication of freshness. Cut or twist the tops off before storing carrots in a plastic bag in the refrigerator, or they will draw moisture from the root. Unfortunately, those tops are only good for the compost pile. Carrots will keep for several weeks in the refrigerator.

SIMPLE PREPARATION: It's important to clean carrots well before eating them. Bacteria from the soil may still be present on the surface of the skin. If the carrots are young and tender, there is no need to peel—simply give the carrots a good scrubbing with a stout vegetable brush. If the carrots are older or larger, you may prefer to peel them for aesthetic reasons, since the skins can turn brownish in cooking. Of course, carrots are delicious raw. The fun part is how to prepare them—sticks, rounds, diagonally, julienned, grated, or left whole. They are a favorite vegetable dipper and salad addition. Grated carrots are a salad in themselves with the addition of a little yogurt and a handful of raisins. Lightly steamed and garnished with snips of fresh chives, there couldn't be an easier vegetable to prepare. In stir-fry dishes, carrots are most beautiful in thin strips or slender slices cut on the diagonal.

For a festive holiday vegetable, prepare this quick and easy dish with dried cranberries.

Carrot Apple Bake

    3 medium carrots, grated
    1 tart apple, grated
    ¾ cup chopped dried fruit*
    1 tablespoon maple syrup
    ½ cup apple juice*
    2 teaspoons butter (optional)

Preheat oven to 350°F. Toss carrots, apples, dried fruit, maple syrup, and juice together. Place in a medium-sized oiled casserole dish. Dot with butter. Bake, covered, for approximately 35 minutes or until carrots are just tender-crisp. Serves 6 to 8.

*Different combinations of fruit and juice change the character of this recipe. If you use sweet dried fruit such as prunes or dried apples, with apple juice for the liquid, this dish will be quite sweet. Dried cranberries and orange juice make it more tart.

Nutrition information per serving, 6 servings per recipe: Calories: 117. Protein: 1g. Total fat: <1g (sat. fat: <1g). Carbohydrates: 26g. Cholesterol: 1.7mg. Sodium: 24mg. Vitamin A: 108% DV. Vitamin C: 10% DV.

For anyone who's had trouble cooking brown rice, here's a dependable and tasty variation. It's important to use a good, flavorful stock to make this recipe.

Baked Brown Rice with Carrots

    1 tablespoon canola oil
    ½ cup chopped onion
    1½ to 2 cups coarsely grated carrot
    2 cups long grain brown rice
    ½ cup finely chopped parsley
    4 cups clear vegetable soup stock or broth

Preheat oven to 350°F. Heat oil in heavy skillet over medium heat. Add onions and carrots. Sauté for 5 minutes. Add rice and sauté briefly until rice is evenly coated with oil. Toss in parsley. Add broth. Place mixture in a medium-sized casserole and bake, covered, for 50 minutes or until liquid is absorbed and rice is tender. Serves 6 to 8.

Nutrition information per serving, 6 servings per recipe: Calories: 361. Protein: 10g. Total fat: 3.3g (sat. fat: <1g). Carbohydrates: 70g. Cholesterol: 0mg. Sodium: 212mg. Vitamin A: 120% DV. Vitamin C: 16% DV.

Freezing tofu dramatically changes its normally soft personality. Tofu that has been frozen is quite chewy and easily absorbs marinade. It is just perfect in this hearty Peasant Pie. For a very special treat, line your baking pan with a whole wheat pie crust.

Tofu Peasant Pie

2 pounds tofu, frozen and then thawed
4 tablespoons reduced-sodium soy sauce
2 tablespoons canola oil
5 cloves garlic, minced or pressed
1½ cups chopped onions
1½ cups chopped celery
1½ cups sliced carrots
4 to 5 medium-sized potatoes, cubed
salt and milk to make mashed potatoes

Squeeze thawed tofu to remove excess water. Cut into ½-inch cubes and place in medium-sized bowl. Mix together the soy sauce, oil, and 2 cloves of the garlic. Pour this mixture over tofu cubes, tossing lightly to distribute evenly. In a large skillet, lightly brown tofu cubes over medium heat for approximately 10 minutes, using a stiff metal spatula to turn the pieces. If necessary, use a small amount of oil or broth to prevent sticking. Set aside. Steam onions, celery, carrots, and the remaining 3 cloves of garlic, until just tender. While vegetables are steaming, boil potatoes. When potatoes are soft, drain and mash, adding salt to taste and milk to create desired consistency. Now you're ready to assemble. Preheat oven to 350°F. Toss tofu with the steamed vegetables. Place in an oiled 9 x 13-inch baking dish. Cover evenly with the mashed potatoes. Bake for 45 minutes. Serves 8.

Nutrition information per serving, 8 servings per recipe: Calories: 236. Protein: 12g. Total fat: 8.5g (sat. fat: 1g). Carbohydrates: 26g. Cholesterol: 0.5mg. Sodium: 421mg. Vitamin A: 41% DV. Vitamin C: 30% DV.

Besides being the ultimate raw vegetable, and an integral part of salads and stews and casseroles of all sorts, carrots display yet another aspect of their versatile personality in moist and sweet carrot cake.

Maple Buttermilk Carrot Cake

2 eggs, beaten
½ cup canola oil
½ cup maple syrup
½ cup buttermilk
1¼ cups whole wheat pastry flour
½ teaspoon salt
1 teaspoon baking soda
1 tablespoon cinnamon
1½ cups finely grated carrots

Preheat oven to 300°F. Mix eggs, oil, maple syrup, and buttermilk together in a medium-sized mixing bowl. Sift in the flour, salt, and baking soda and mix well. Stir in the carrots. Pour batter into an oiled 8 x 8-inch baking pan. Bake for approximately 45 minutes or until golden and firm to the touch. Serves 9.

Nutrition information per serving, 9 servings per recipe: Calories: 238. Protein: 4g. Total fat: 13g (sat. fat: 1.4g). Carbohydrates: 25g. Cholesterol: 37mg. Sodium: 245mg. Vitamin A: 55% DV. Vitamin C: 4% DV.

NUTRITION INFORMATION PER LARGE CARROT, RAW:

Calories: 31
Total fat: 0g
(saturated fat: 0g)
Fiber: 1.8g
Sodium: 25mg
Potassium: 7% Daily Value
Vitamin A: 203% Daily Value
Vitamin C: 12% Daily Value
Iron: 2% Daily Value
Calcium: 2% Daily Value

CARROTS

CAULIFLOWER

CAULIFLOWER
was brought to Europe when Spain was invaded by the Moors. This attractive vegetable, once thought to be purely ornamental, derives its common name from the Italian *cavolfiore*, loosely translated to mean "the cabbage that blooms like a flower." Cauliflower is yet another member of the Brassicaeae or mustard family and is therefore related to all those powerful veggies like broccoli and turnips. Most of us are familiar with the snowy-white variety of cauliflower, but there is also a purple-headed type as well as a chartreuse variety—both are a cross between cauliflower and broccoli.

HANDLING: Fresh cauliflower is a creamy or snowy-white color, very firm, with fresh green leaves around the outside of the head. Cauliflower is best eaten soon after harvesting—its flavor grows stronger with storage. Be sure to let your cauliflower have some breathing room in the refrigerator—store loosely wrapped in perforated plastic or an unsealed bag. Wash the surface of the cauliflower head and trim off discolored areas before cooking. Cut away the thick bottom end and cut out the core. You're ready to steam the cauliflower, whole or broken into florets.

SIMPLE PREPARATION: Raw cauliflower is excellent on fresh vegetable platters and will hold up well with the thickest of dips. If you prefer your cauliflower cooked, you really need only a light steaming—be very careful to not overcook. Overcooking causes the breakdown of sulphur compounds in cauliflower, releasing a stronger than normal odor to an already hardy-smelling veggie. Most cooks break or cut cauliflower up into individual florets for cooking, but it is just as easy and quite attractive to steam or blanch the head in one piece after removing the core. Simply put the whole cauliflower, head side up, in the steamer basket and cook until just tender. Carefully slip the cooked head onto a serving plate and drizzle with lemon butter, simple white sauce, or cheese sauce.

Here's a flavorful dish that combines cauliflower with tomatoes, herbs, and chili flakes for a wonderful pasta sauce that's got a little kick.

Spicy Cauliflower Sauce over Rigatoni

1 pound rigatoni noodles
1 tablespoon olive oil
1 tablespoon fresh oregano (or 1 teaspoon dried oregano)
1 medium onion, cut in slivers (approximately 1½ cups)
3 cloves garlic, pressed or minced
¾ to 1 teaspoon dried chili flakes
1 medium head cauliflower cut into small florets, (approximately 6 cups)
1 large green pepper, cut into small slivers
¾ teaspoon salt
½ cup dry red wine, broth, or water
28-ounce can diced tomatoes
freshly ground black pepper to taste
¼ cup chopped fresh parsley
2 to 4 tablespoons chopped fresh cilantro (optional)
freshly grated Asiago cheese

Put on a large pot of water and cook the pasta while you prepare the sauce. Heat oil in a large, deep skillet or heavy soup pot over medium heat. Add the oregano, onions, garlic, and chili flakes. Sauté for 3 minutes. Add cauliflower, green peppers, and salt. Sauté for 2 more minutes. Add the red wine, broth, or water, cover and steam for approximately 10 minutes, or until cauliflower is just barely tender. Add tomatoes and black pepper and simmer, uncovered, for 10 more minutes. Turn off the heat. Toss in the parsley and cilantro. Pile hot, cooked rigatoni on a very large, deep platter. Top with cauliflower sauce. Pass the Asiago cheese to sprinkle on top. Serves 8.

Nutrition information per serving, 8 servings per recipe: Calories: 135. Protein: 5g. Total fat: 2g (sat. fat: <1g). Carbohydrates: 24g. Cholesterol: 0mg. Sodium: 311mg. Vitamin A: 19% DV. Vitamin C: 145% DV.

Potatoes, cauliflower, and Cheddar cheese are perfect together in this friendly soup.

Cauliflower Cheese Chowder

1 tablespoon canola oil
1 medium onion, chopped
3 cloves garlic, minced or pressed
2 tablespoons unbleached white flour
4 cups vegetable stock or water
1 medium head cauliflower, cut into small florets
2 medium potatoes, unpeeled, cut into cubes
¾ teaspoon salt
½ cup skim milk
1 cup grated reduced-fat Cheddar cheese
freshly ground black pepper
freshly grated nutmeg to taste
snips of fresh chives for garnish (optional)

Heat oil in soup pot over medium heat. Add onion and garlic and sauté until tender, approximately 10 minutes. Stir often to avoid scorching. Add flour, stirring constantly for 1 minute. Slowly add stock or water, using a whisk if necessary to avoid lumps. Add cauliflower, potatoes, and salt. Bring just to a boil, reduce heat, cover, and simmer until vegetables are tender, approximately 20 minutes. Remove about half of the cauliflower and potatoes from the pot using a slotted spoon. Set aside. Let the remaining soup cool just a bit and then purée the soup in a food processor, blender, or right in the pot using a hand-held blender. Return soup to pot, add reserved cauliflower and potatoes. Heat to a simmer. Slowly whisk in milk, then grated cheese. Heat over low heat until cheese is melted. Season with black pepper and a small amount of nutmeg. Serve embellished with a sprinkle of freshly snipped chives. Serves 4.

Nutrition information per serving, 4 servings per recipe: Calories: 231. Protein: 10g. Total fat: 7.6g (sat. fat: 2.6g). Carbohydrates: 28g. Cholesterol: 15.5mg. Sodium: 601mg. Vitamin A: 7% DV. Vitamin C: 222% DV.

NUTRITION INFORMATION PER ½ CUP CAULIFLOWER, COOKED:

Calories: 15
Total fat: <0.2g
   (saturated fat: 0g)
Fiber: 1.1g
Sodium: 4mg
Potassium: 6% Daily Value
Vitamin A: <1% Daily Value
Vitamin C: 57% Daily Value
Iron: 2% Daily Value
Calcium: 2% Daily Value

CAULIFLOWER

CHINESE CABBAGE

CHINESE CABBAGE, also known as Napa, Chinese Celery cabbage, or a
host of other familiar and unfamiliar names, refers broadly to that group of *Brassica* that are
thinner-leafed than the more common head cabbage. The type of Chinese cabbage we're
referring to here usually is a pale green, upright head with fanned out, highly veined, almost
crinkled leaves. Chinese cabbage is juicy, tender, and much more mild than regular head
cabbage—so much so that you may even be able to convince a hesitant cabbage-eater to enjoy
it either raw or cooked into a delicious stir-fry.

HANDLING: Chinese cabbage heads are often fairly large, which is okay since this watery
vegetable cooks down considerably. It also stores well in the refrigerator, so if you have half a
head left over you'll have time to make up another creative use for it. Your cabbage should have
a somewhat firm head with no signs of browning. Keep the cabbage stored in a sealed plastic
bag—it will keep for up to two weeks if you're going to use it in a cooked dish. Eat it sooner if
you want it crisp and raw for salads or dippers.

SIMPLE PREPARATION: Separate leaves from the stalk and rinse carefully to remove soil and
debris. Cut ribbons of the whole leaf to add to salads or as a last-minute addition to delicate
clear broths and soups. For dipping, trim the leaves from the stalks and use like celery. You can
prepare Chinese cabbage as a simple side dish by lightly stir-frying ribbons or large pieces of
the whole leaf in a bit of hot sesame or peanut oil along with some crushed or minced garlic.
Sprinkle lightly with soy sauce and stir until just wilted but still tender-crisp.

Seitan adds a rich, deep taste to this vegetable stir-fry. Seitan, also called "wheat meat," is made from the glutenous part of wheat. It is very high in protein and extremely low in fat, with no cholesterol. Seitan is available in the refrigerated section of natural food stores and some Oriental markets.

Chop Suey with Seitan

1 tablespoon peanut oil
1 large onion, cut into crescents
3 cloves garlic, minced or pressed
8 ounces seitan, cut in strips
1 carrot, cut in matchsticks
3 stalks celery, cut on the diagonal
1 red or green pepper, cut into strips
3 to 4 cups Chinese cabbage, thinly sliced
1½ cups snap peas, whole or cut on the diagonal
1 tablespoon soy sauce
1 teaspoon molasses
black pepper to taste
1 cup mung bean sprouts

Heat oil in large, deep skillet or wok over medium-high heat. Add onions and garlic. Stir-fry for 2 minutes. Add seitan, carrots, and celery. Stir-fry for 2 more minutes. Add green or red pepper, Chinese cabbage, and snap peas. Stir-fry 1 more minute. Add soy sauce, drizzle on the molasses, and add plenty of black pepper. Continue cooking, stirring often, over medium-high heat until veggies are just tender-crisp, approximately 10 minutes. Just before serving, stir in bean sprouts. Serve on a bed of hot basmati rice. Pass the soy sauce for extra seasoning if desired. Serves 6 to 8.

Nutrition information per serving, 6 servings per recipe: Calories: 118. Protein: 13g. Total fat: 2.2g (sat. fat: <1g). Carbohydrates: 18g. Cholesterol: 0mg. Sodium: 233mg. Vitamin A: 47% DV. Vitamin C: 105% DV.

The sweetness of golden raisins contrasts with the heat of hot pepper flakes in this quick and easy stir-fry featuring Chinese cabbage. How much hot pepper you use is up to your taste and tolerance—it is quite delicious when slightly scorching hot. Serve with basmati rice as a side dish to accompany barbequed tempeh or pan-fried tofu.

Spicy and Sweet Chinese Cabbage

1 tablespoon peanut oil
1½ pounds Chinese cabbage, thinly sliced (8 to 10 cups)
2 teaspoons finely grated ginger root
crushed hot pepper flakes to taste
¼ cup golden raisins, soaked in ½ cup warm water, then drained
1 tablespoon honey or brown sugar
1 tablespoon cider vinegar
½ teaspoon salt

Heat oil in deep skillet or wok over medium-high heat. Add Chinese cabbage, ginger, and hot pepper flakes. Stir-fry for 2 minutes, stirring constantly. Reduce heat to medium. Mix sweetener and vinegar. Pour over cabbage mixture. Toss in raisins, season with salt. Cook for approximately 3 more minutes, stirring often. Cabbage should be wilted but still slightly crunchy. Serve immediately. Serves 4.

Nutrition information per serving, 4 servings per recipe: Calories: 97. Protein: 1g. Total fat: 3.2g (sat. fat: <1g). Carbohydrates: 14g. Cholesterol: 0mg. Sodium: 361mg. Vitamin A: 43% DV. Vitamin C: 109% DV.

NUTRITION INFORMATION PER ½ CUP CHINESE CABBAGE, COOKED:

Calories: 8
Total fat: 0g
    (saturated fat: 0g)
Fiber: 0.9g
Sodium: 6mg
Potassium: 4% Daily Value
Vitamin A: 6% Daily Value
Vitamin C: 15% Daily Value
Iron: <1% Daily Value
Calcium: 2% Daily Value

CHINESE CABBAGE

SWEET CORN

CORN
hardly needs an introduction. Who hasn't enjoyed that uniquely American food—corn on the cob? Corn, or maize—its proper name and a word of Native American origin—was one of the first native foods the Pilgrims learned to cultivate and eat. It is also a central part of the cuisines of Mexico, South America, and northern Italy (where it is used for polenta). Sweet corn is actually harvested when it is still immature and the natural sugars have not yet been converted to starches. Best to get your pot of boiling water and bring it out to the field so that you can take your corn right from the stalk to the pot for the absolutely sweetest taste.

HANDLING: Fresh corn on the cob should be eaten soon after harvesting if you want to enjoy the very best flavor—the natural sugars in corn begin converting to starch almost immediately after harvest. If you can't eat your corn right away, get it into the refrigerator quickly and leave it in its husks. If you want to freeze corn for a winter treat, or use it cut off the cob in a chowder or salad, you have to choose between cutting or scraping. Cutting is easy. After husking and removing any bad spots or worms, cut the kernels off the cob with a sharp knife, leaving ⅛ to ¼-inch of pulp on the cob. Cutting yields individual kernels which are best for salads. If you're going to use the corn for chowders or corn pudding, scrape the corn off the cob. First run a knife down the center of a row of kernels all around the cob. Using the back of a knife, scrape both corn and pulp off the cob. You will have corn pieces as well as the fleshy "milk".

SIMPLE PREPARATION: Corn's finest preparation is also the very simplest. Husk the outer leaves from the corn and remove the strands of silk that cling to the ear. Cut out any bad spots, including the worm you'll occasionally see at the top of an ear. Steaming takes 6 to 10 minutes; boiling takes about 4 to 7 minutes. If you're having a cookout, corn on the cob can be cooked on the grill. Pull down the outer husks without detaching. Remove the silk, then pull husks back up around the cob. Soak whole cobs in water for 10 minutes before placing on hot grill. Turn several times during grilling, which should take approximately 15 minutes. If you're using corn cut off the cob for a salad, steam the kernels first for 4 to 5 minutes.

This is a salad that's well worth the time it takes to cook a pot of barley. Fresh corn, bell peppers, and a light vinaigrette are wonderful in combination with this chewy grain.

Corn and Barley Salad

2 cups corn (fresh off the cob, or frozen)
2 cups cooked pearled barley*
½ to ¾ cup chopped green bell pepper
½ to ¾ cup chopped red bell pepper
2 green onions, chopped
1 tablespoon chopped fresh cilantro
2 tablespoons canola oil
2 tablespoons freshly-squeezed lemon juice
½ teaspoon salt
freshly ground black pepper to taste

If using fresh corn, cut corn from the cob and steam or boil kernels for several minutes until tender. If using frozen corn, steam until thoroughly thawed. In a large bowl mix all ingredients together. For a more lively salad, add minced fresh hot pepper or dried red pepper flakes. Serve cold or at room temperature with big wedges of fresh tomato. This salad keeps very well for several days in the refrigerator. Serves 6.

*Barley is a chewy, easily digestible grain which is often overlooked. Like most whole grains, barley takes about an hour to cook but requires very little attention during the process. "Pearled" refers to the process of removing the hull through the abrasive action of pearling machines. Barley is also delicious in soups and stews, and quite good mixed with apples and sweetener to create a fine baked pudding.

Nutrition information per serving, 6 servings per recipe: Calories: 158. Protein: 3g. Total fat: 4.7g (sat. fat <1g). Carbohydrates: 26g. Cholesterol: 0mg. Sodium: 183mg. Vitamin A: 12% DV. Vitamin C: 81% DV.

Stuffing isn't just a holiday food. It is a wonderful side dish for any meal—especially in the middle of the summer when fresh corn is in season.

Summer Corn Stuffing

1 tablespoon butter or canola oil
2 stalks celery, chopped
1 green pepper, chopped
1 red pepper, chopped
1 small onion, chopped
3 tablespoons chopped fresh parsley
½ teaspoon salt
freshly ground black pepper to taste
¼ teaspoon dried sage
2 cups corn kernels, cooked
8 cups dry, cubed bread*
3 to 4 cups vegetable broth

Preheat oven to 350°F. Heat butter or oil in a large skillet over medium heat. Add celery, green and red peppers, and onion. Sauté until tender. Turn off heat and mix in parsley, salt, pepper, sage, and corn. In a large casserole dish, mix bread cubes with sautéed vegetables. Pour broth over mixture and toss lightly. Bake, covered, for 30 minutes or until heated through. Serves 6.

*French bread makes a tender, light stuffing. For a heartier and satisfying dish use whole wheat bread.

Nutrition information per serving, 6 servings per recipe: Calories: 224. Protein: 6g. Total fat: 4.4g (sat. fat: <1g). Carbohydrates: 40g. Cholesterol: <1mg. Sodium: 460mg. Vitamin A: 20% DV. Vitamin C: 78% DV.

Fun, colorful, and a perfect potluck dish!

MexiKansas Pasta Salad

8 to 10 ounces frozen cheese-filled pasta
1½ cups corn kernels, lightly steamed
1 red or green bell pepper, diced
2 to 4 green onions, sliced on the diagonal
¼ cup chopped fresh basil
⅛ to ¼ cup chopped fresh cilantro
¼ cup chopped fresh parsley
juice of 1 lime
1 tablespoon balsamic vinegar
2 tablespoons olive oil
black pepper to taste
½ teaspoon salt
¼ teaspoon ground cumin
¼ to ½ teaspoon crushed red chili peppers

Cook pasta according to package directions. Thoroughly rinse and cool to room temperature. Mix cooled pasta with corn, bell pepper, onions, basil, cilantro, and parsley. Whisk lime juice, vinegar, oil, black pepper, salt, cumin, and chili peppers together and pour over salad. Toss carefully until pasta is well coated. Chill. Toss again before serving. Serves 6.

Nutrition information per serving, 6 servings per recipe: Calories: 209. Protein: 8g. Total fat: 6.2g (sat. fat: 1.8g). Carbohydrates: 29g. Cholesterol: 27mg. Sodium: 371mg. Vitamin A: 9% DV. Vitamin C: 43% DV.

NUTRITION INFORMATION PER 1 EAR CORN, COOKED:

Calories: 83
Total fat: 0.8g
  (saturated fat: <0.2g)
Fiber: 4.4g
Sodium: 13mg
Potassium: 5% Daily Value
Vitamin A: <1% Daily Value
Vitamin C: 8% Daily Value
Iron: 3% Daily Value
Calcium: <1% Daily Value

SWEET CORN

CUCUMBERS

CUCUMBERS have most-favored-vegetable status at our house. Easy to grow, easy to eat, the perfect accompaniment to any summer meal, better than lettuce on sandwiches. We must be following in the footsteps of the Roman emperor Tiberius who supposedly ate 10 cucumbers daily. Cukes have been around, and popular, for a long, long time. A member of the gourd and squash family, they have been cultivated in India, Egypt, Asia, and Europe, and traveled to the Americas, where we enjoy many different varieties. Our family favorite is the Oriental variety—a smooth-skinned, long, narrow, almost seedless variety with a mild taste.

HANDLING: Cucumbers should be medium or deep green, and very solid. Store them in the vegetable drawer in the refrigerator and plan to eat them within several days—they are at their best when fresh from the garden. Some varieties keep a little better than others. The Oriental variety, unfortunately, goes limp quickly, which is why you sometimes see them shrink-wrapped in plastic. More traditional cukes aren't quite so thin and are better keepers. Pickling varieties are the plumpest and shortest of all. Never settle for oversized or yellow-tinged cukes—the seeds will be big and the taste bitter.

SIMPLE PREPARATION: Scrub well, slice, and enjoy. That's the simplest preparation if your cukes are fresh and the skins aren't bitter. Sometimes when the weather's been hot or dry cucumber skins get a little tough or bitter, and then it's best to peel. If a cucumber is large and seedy you also might want to cut it lengthwise and scrape the seeds out. Although most of us think of cucumbers as a fresh, raw vegetable, you can also cook them. Peeled, seeded cucumber pieces can be sautéed lightly in butter and served with chopped fresh dill for a quick summer vegetable side dish.

There's a time in the summer when potatoes, green beans, and cucumbers are all plentiful at the same time. Here's what you make with the bounty.

Potato Salad with Green Beans and Cukes

1 pound waxy potatoes
2½ cups fresh green beans
1 cucumber, seeded and chopped
¼ cup chopped red onion
2 tablespoons minced fresh dill weed
2 tablespoons olive oil
2 tablespoons freshly squeezed lemon juice
¾ teaspoon salt
black pepper to taste
1 teaspoon sugar or honey
1 teaspoon Dijon mustard

Wash potatoes. Boil whole, unpeeled potatoes until just barely tender. Allow to cool while you prepare the green beans. Cut beans in half with a diagonal cut. Steam lightly. Immediately rinse under cool water to stop their cooking. Cut potatoes into chunks. Toss together the potatoes, beans, cucumber, red onion, and dill weed. Whisk together the olive oil, lemon juice, salt, pepper, sweetener, and mustard. Toss carefully with potato mixture. Refrigerate for several hours. Toss salad again before serving. Serves 6.

Nutrition information per serving, 6 servings per recipe: Calories: 139. Protein: 2g. Total fat: 4.5g (sat. fat: <1g). Carbohydrates: 22g. Cholesterol: 0mg. Sodium: 296mg. Vitamin A: 4% DV. Vitamin C: 34% DV.

Summers can get pretty nasty in Kansas. Definitely too hot to turn on the oven. Sometimes too hot to even turn on a burner. That's when this cooling soup is most delicious. Serve with crusty dark bread and a selection of cheeses and fruit for a light meal on a hot summer day.

Chilly Cucumber Soup

4 cups plain nonfat yogurt
2 cups minced cucumbers*
1 red bell pepper, finely minced
1 tablespoon mild-tasting vinegar, preferably white
2 to 3 cloves garlic, finely minced or pressed
1 to 2 tablespoons finely chopped fresh mint
1 tablespoon chopped fresh dill weed (or 1 teaspoon dried)
1 teaspoon salt
lots of freshly ground black pepper

Mix all ingredients together well. Chill for at least 3 hours. Mix again before serving. Serves 6.

*If you're using unwaxed, organically grown cucumbers, there's no need to peel them as long as the skins aren't bitter. The dark bits of skin will add color and texture. If you prefer the soup very delicate in color and texture, or are using waxed cukes, then go ahead and peel them before mincing.

Nutrition information per serving, 6 servings per recipe: Calories: 104. Protein: 11g. Total fat: <1g (sat. fat: <1g). Carbohydrates: 15g. Cholesterol: 3mg. Sodium: 486mg. Vitamin A: 8% DV. Vitamin C: 45% DV.

Serve this spicy and flavorful relish with rice and beans, as an accompaniment to an Indian dinner, or as a dip with tortilla chips as part of a Mexican feast.

Sassy Corn and Cucumber Relish

    1 cup fresh corn kernels, steamed
    1 cucumber, seeded and diced
    2 green onions, finely chopped
    2 teaspoons sugar or honey
    ½ teaspoon salt
    3 to 4 teaspoons finely chopped cilantro
    1 tablespoon red wine vinegar or balsamic vinegar
    1 tablespoon sesame oil
    1 teaspoon dried red chili flakes
    1 small hot pepper, seeded and minced

Mix all ingredients. Refrigerate for several hours to allow flavors to blend. Serves 8 to 10 as a condiment.

Nutrition information per serving, 8 servings per recipe: Calories: 62. Protein: 1g. Total fat: 1.8g (sat. fat: <1g). Carbohydrates: 10g. Cholesterol: 0mg. Sodium: 141mg. Vitamin A: 4% DV. Vitamin C: 34% DV.

NUTRITION INFORMATION PER ½ CUP CUCUMBER, RAW:

Calories: 7
Total fat: 0g
    (saturated fat: 0g)
Fiber: 0.7g
Sodium: 1mg
Potassium: 2% Daily Value
Vitamin A: <1% Daily Value
Vitamin C: 3% Daily Value
Iron: <1% Daily Value
Calcium: <1% Daily Value

DAIKON RADISH, also known as Oriental radish, Japanese radish, or
Chinese radish, is a vegetable still finding its place in the American market. These long, white roots with a relatively mild taste are a member of the same family as the round, more familiar bright red radishes. In many parts of the East, daikon radishes, either cooked, raw, or pickled, are served with nearly all meals. Part of daikon's charm is its ability to be carved into beautiful and sometimes elaborate garnishes.

HANDLING: Daikon radishes are not as hardy as you might think. They lose their moisture over time and can become limp—store them in the refrigerator wrapped in plastic, especially if you want to use them raw and crisp. If you'll be cooking your radishes you can store daikon for up to a week.

SIMPLE PREPARATION: A simple scrubbing is enough for daikon radishes. Unless they are extremely large or a little more mature, the skin is thin and tender and doesn't require peeling. If you're going to use your radish raw in a salad or as a condiment, just grate and toss with oil and vinegar, salt, a touch of sweetener, and other veggies if you'd like. Daikon slices can be sautéed in a bit of oil and lightly seasoned with salt and fresh herbs. Cooking disarms daikon's slight bite, creating a dish with a taste like mild turnips.

Here's an attractive relish that's easy to make. Enjoy the simplicity of the white, green, and red veggies in this fresh and light condiment. Create a rich and creamy taste with the addition of lowfat yogurt or light sour cream—delicious served with Indian cuisine or to embellish a meal of beans and rice.

Daikon Relish

¼ cup finely chopped onion
¼ cup finely chopped red bell pepper
¼ cup finely chopped green bell pepper
½ cup coarsely grated daikon radish
¼ teaspoon salt
cayenne pepper to taste
1 tablespoon lemon juice
½ cup lowfat yogurt or light sour cream (optional)

Combine all ingredients. Allow flavors to blend for several hours in the refrigerator before serving. Makes approximately 1½ cups.

Nutrition information per ¼ cup serving, 6 servings per recipe, prepared with lowfat yogurt: Calories: 20. Protein: 1g. Total fat: <1g (sat. fat: <1g). Carbohydrates: 3g. Cholesterol: 1.3mg. Sodium: 106mg. Vitamin A: 3%DV. Vitamin C: 28% DV.

Tame daikon's bite with a quick stir-frying.

Stir-fried Daikon

1 pound daikon radish
1 tablespoon peanut oil
1 teaspoon sweetener of your choice
⅛ teaspoon salt
2 tablespoons finely chopped parsley

Scrub daikon and cut in thin slices. Heat oil in a heavy skillet or wok over medium-high heat. Add daikon and toss to coat with oil. Sprinkle sweetener and salt over radish slices. Cook, stirring often, until radishes are just tender—about 5 minutes. Remove from heat. Toss in parsley. Serve immediately. Serves 3.

Nutrition information per serving, 3 servings per recipe: Calories: 75. Protein: 1g. Total fat: 4.6g (sat. fat: <1g). Carbohydrates: 7g. Cholesterol: 0mg. Sodium: 110mg. Vitamin A: 1% DV. Vitamin C: 41% DV.

Rice vinegar and sesame oil, combined with a touch of sweetener and soy sauce, create a savory dressing for this vegetable salad featuring daikon, cucumbers, and zucchini.

Zucchini and Daikon Salad

2 small zucchini
½ cucumber, seeded and chopped
½ pound daikon, thinly sliced
1 medium red, green, or yellow bell pepper, chopped
1 tablespoon soy sauce
1 teaspoon sweetener
2 tablespoons rice vinegar
1 tablespoon canola oil
1 tablespoon sesame oil

Cut zucchini in thin slices. Drop briefly in boiling water to lightly blanch. Immediately rinse in cool water. Drain well. Zucchini should be just barely tender but not limp or soft. Toss zucchini with cucumber, daikon slices, and bell pepper. Whisk or shake remaining ingredients together until well blended. Pour over vegetables and toss carefully. Chill for several hours. Toss again before serving. Serves 4 to 6.

Nutrition information per serving, 4 servings per recipe: Calories: 95. Protein: 1g. Total fat: 6.6g (sat. fat: <1g). Carbohydrates: 7g. Cholesterol: 0mg. Sodium: 161mg. Vitamin A: 3% DV. Vitamin C: 64% DV.

NUTRITION INFORMATION PER ½ CUP DAIKON RADISH, RAW:

Calories: 8
Total fat: 0g
         (saturated fat: 0g)
Fiber: 1g
Sodium: 9mg
Potassium: 3% Daily Value
Vitamin A: 0% Daily Value
Vitamin C: 17% Daily Value
Iron: 1% Daily Value
Calcium: 1% Daily Value

DAIKON

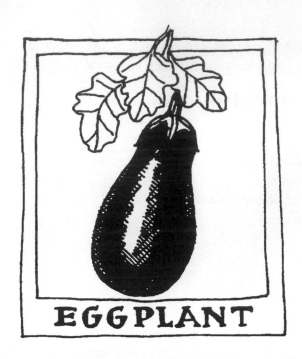

EGGPLANT

EGGPLANT is a gorgeous, sensual-looking vegetable that remains somewhat

mysterious to many cooks. Eggplant is a member of the Solanaceae, or nightshade family, and
is therefore related to potatoes and tomatoes as well as being connected to the more ominous
belladonna, horse nettle, and tobacco. Long a staple in parts of the East and the Mediterranean,
eggplant is an important ingredient in cuisines where meat plays a more secondary role. Its
texture is fleshy and substantive, providing an excellent base for rich-tasting dishes such as
Baba Ganoush and Ratatouille.

HANDLING: Eggplants would rather be eaten than stored. If you need to keep them for
several days you will have to deal with their rather demanding needs—they dislike both hot and
cold temperatures. Ideally you would store eggplant in a cool place (about 50°F), wrapped in
plastic. If the weather is extremely hot, you can keep eggplant in the refrigerator, but it tends to
develop brown spots and a slightly bitter taste after several days.

SIMPLE PREPARATION: Before you do anything with eggplant you have to decide whether or
not to peel it. If your eggplant is fresh, young, and tender, you can leave the skins on if you'd
like the added color and texture in your dish. If the eggplant is large or if you simply prefer
eggplant peeled, by all means peel it. You can cube eggplant and sauté it in olive oil until
tender. Season with salt, pepper,and herbs such as basil, thyme, or rosemary. You can also slice
eggplant into ½ to ¾-inch slices, brush with olive oil, and bake in a 425°F oven until tender
(5 to 10 minutes). Top with buttered bread crumbs, a spread of pesto or herbed butter and broil
until nicely browned. When cooking eggplant, keep in mind that it will absorb as much oil as
you are willing to use, so be prudent when measuring out the oil—remembering that every level
tablespoon of oil contains 14 grams of fat.

Ratatouille is a wonderful blend of summer produce, cooked to create a thick, chunky sauce. Here it is served on top of a layer of cheese-filled pasta for a one-dish dinner.

Ratatouille Bake

1 tablespoon olive oil
3 to 5 cloves garlic, minced or pressed
1 medium onion, chopped
2 cups eggplant, peeled and diced
2 cups zucchini (or other summer squash), chopped
1 large green or red pepper, diced
2 to 3 medium tomatoes, chopped
2 tablespoons chopped fresh parsley
2 tablespoons chopped fresh basil
½ teaspoon salt
⅛ teaspoon black pepper
8 to 10 ounce package frozen cheese-filled pasta (ravioli or tortelloni)
4 ounces Mozzarella cheese, grated

Heat oil in heavy skillet over medium heat. Add garlic, onions, and eggplant and sauté for several minutes, stirring constantly. Add zucchini, pepper, tomatoes, parsley, basil, salt, and pepper. Stir well and cook over medium heat several minutes more. Reduce heat to simmer and allow to cook until vegetables are tender and flavors are well blended, approximately 30 minutes. While vegetables are simmering, cook pasta according to package directions. Drain well. Lightly oil a large casserole and line bottom with cooked pasta. Cover with hot vegetables (ratatouille). Top with grated cheese. Broil until nicely brown on top. Serves 6.

Nutrition information per serving, 6 servings per recipe: Calories: 231. Protein: 12g. Total fat: 10.6g (sat. fat: 5.8g). Carbohydrates: 20g. Cholesterol: 54mg. Sodium: 465mg. Vitamin A: 16% DV. Vitamin C: 59% DV.

Eggplant takes the place of noodles in this lasagna dish, creating a slightly different version of a popular recipe.

Eggplant Lasagna

1 cup bread crumbs
¼ cup Parmesan cheese
1 large eggplant, peeled, cut into ½-inch-thick slices
2 egg whites, beaten
3 tablespoons olive oil
3 cups pasta sauce (homemade or prepared)
2 cups lowfat Ricotta cheese
4 tablespoons chopped fresh parsley
freshly ground black pepper to taste
1 cup grated Mozzarella cheese

Preheat oven to 350°F. Mix bread crumbs with Parmesan cheese. Dip eggplant slices in beaten egg whites. Coat with breadcrumb mixture. Heat 1 or 2 tablespoons of the oil in a large skillet over medium heat. Most likely you will have to brown the eggplant slices in several batches, so portion out your frying oil according to how many slices of eggplant you can fit in your pan. Lightly brown the coated eggplant slices on both sides. Spoon 1 cup of the pasta sauce in the bottom of a 7 x 12-inch pan. Arrange half of the eggplant slices on top of the sauce. Mix Ricotta with parsley and black pepper. Spoon half of this mixture on top of the eggplant. Repeat layers: sauce, eggplant, Ricotta. End with the remaining cup of sauce. Top with grated Mozzarella. Bake, uncovered, until thoroughly heated, about 35 to 45 minutes. Serves 8.

Nutrition information per serving, 8 servings per recipe: Calories: 287. Protein: 17g. Total fat: 12.2g (sat. fat: 5.1g). Carbohydrates: 26g. Cholesterol: 28mg. Sodium: 308mg. Vitamin A: 48% DV. Vitamin C: 17% DV.

This delicious "caviar" was first introduced to me by my good friend, excellent cook, and dedicated dietician, Chris Ellis. It is wonderful spread on thin rice crackers.

Eggplant Caviar

1 tablespoon olive oil
2 to 3 cloves garlic, pressed or minced
1 medium-sized onion, finely chopped
1 green pepper, chopped
1 small eggplant, chopped (peel if desired)
¼ cup red wine
6-ounce can tomato paste
½ teaspoon salt
½ teaspoon oregano
½ teaspoon black pepper
2 tablespoons wine vinegar
1 tablespoon honey or brown sugar

Heat oil over medium heat in a small saucepan. Briefly sauté garlic and onion. Add green pepper and eggplant. Sauté for several more minutes. Add wine, reduce heat to medium-low, and simmer for 10 minutes. Add the tomato paste, salt, oregano, black pepper, wine vinegar, and sweetener. Cook for another 10 to 15 minutes over low heat. Chill well. Serves 6 to 8.

Nutrition information per serving, 6 servings per recipe: Calories: 94. Protein: 1g. Total fat: 2.3g (sat. fat: <1g). Carbohydrates: 16g. Cholesterol: 0mg. Sodium: 262mg. Vitamin A: 8% DV. Vitamin C: 54% DV.

NUTRITION INFORMATION PER ½ CUP EGGPLANT, COOKED:

Calories: 13
Total fat: <0.2g
   (saturated fat: 0g)
Fiber: 1g
Sodium: 2mg
Potassium: 3% Daily Value
Vitamin A: <1% Daily Value
Vitamin C: 2% Daily Value
Iron: 1% Daily Value
Calcium: <1% Daily Value

EGGPLANT

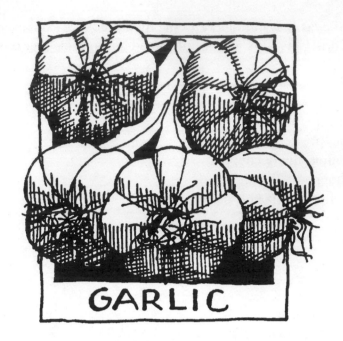

GARLIC

GARLIC,
chives, scallions, shallots, leeks, onions—all are members of the Lily family. And how changed our cuisine would be without their distinctive contributions. Garlic, in particular, is a small but powerful character. Used fresh and raw, garlic can be biting and sharp. Eat too much of it (is there such a thing?) and everyone within ten feet will know what you've consumed. Add some fire to garlic, in the form of roasting or sautéeing, and garlic will be tamed, almost sweetened. Larger Elephant garlic is milder than regular garlic and much easier to prepare since the individual cloves are quite big.

HANDLING: Store bulbs in a cool, dry place.

SIMPLE PREPARATION: Break individual garlic cloves off the base of the head. For easy peeling, press the garlic clove firmly against a cutting board with the flat blade of a knife. This breaks the clove down slightly and the skins slip off easily. Whether to press or mince is up to you. A good garlic press is an invaluable and simple kitchen tool—but you need a sturdy one. Pressing is quick and is best for dishes where you want a puree of garlic rather than little bits. I especially like to use a press if I'm trying to evenly integrate raw garlic into a recipe and I don't want anyone biting into a piece of chopped garlic. The downside of pressing is that you waste some of the garlic pulp and precious juices. Sometimes, especially if you'll be sautéeing garlic, it's preferable to mince or chop. Of course, you can always use whole cloves, especially nice in a long-simmered pot of spaghetti sauce. After slow, long cooking, whole garlic cloves are very mild. Probably the easiest preparation for garlic is baking whole garlic heads to create a buttery, rich spread. Complete directions follow.

This savory salad gets its wonderful flavor from a combination of garlic, fresh ginger, and a hint of sweetness in the marinade. It can be made with any type of rice but I prefer basmati, with its lovely flowery taste.

Marinated Tofu and Basmati Rice Salad

1 cup brown basmati rice, uncooked
4 tablespoons canola oil
3 tablespoons reduced-sodium soy sauce
1 to 3 cloves garlic, minced or pressed
½ tablespoon freshly grated ginger root
1 teaspoon honey
1 pound firm tofu
1 cup peas (if you're using fresh peas, lightly steam them. If you're using frozen peas, just rinse under cool running water—enough to thaw them)
1 carrot, coarsely grated
2 to 3 tablespoons minced onion
several generous grinds of black pepper

Wash rice well. Place in a saucepan with 2 cups water. Bring to a full boil. Boil for three minutes. Cover and reduce to a simmer. Cook for 45 minutes without stirring. Remove from heat. Let sit for 10 to 15 minutes. Transfer to a medium-sized bowl. Lightly fluff with a fork. Allow to cool to room temperature. While the rice is cooking, mix 2 tablespoons of the oil, soy sauce, garlic, ginger root, and honey in a medium-sized bowl. Set aside. Prepare tofu by draining and patting dry with a towel. Cut tofu into long, thin strips approximately ¼ by ¼-inch thick and 2 to 3-inches long. Fry these little strips in the remaining 2 tablespoons of oil over medium-high heat until they're golden and slightly shriveled. A wok works best for this. If you use a frying pan you will need to keep a close eye on the tofu so it doesn't stick. Drain the tofu strips on a paper towel to remove excess oil. Add tofu to the bowl with the marinade and toss lightly until strips are well coated. Allow to marinate for 15 to 20 minutes. Mix the peas, carrots, and onion in with the cooked, cooled rice. Toss in the tofu and its marinade. Add the black pepper. Mix all together well. Allow to chill in refrigerator for at least a couple of hours before serving. This dish just gets better with time. Serves 8.

Nutrition information per serving, 8 servings per recipe: Calories: 183. Protein: 7g. Total fat: 9.1g (sat. fat: <1g). Carbohydrates: 18g. Cholesterol: 0mg. Sodium: 234mg. Vitamin A: 27% DV. Vitamin C: 7% DV.

The first time someone suggested roasting garlic to me, I couldn't imagine how strong the smell would be. Actually, it is very mild—both in aroma and taste. Use roasted garlic as a spread for bread, on pasta, in soups, or mashed in with potatoes.

Roasted Garlic

1 head garlic
1 teaspoon olive oil
sprigs of thyme (optional)

Preheat oven to 250°F. Remove the outermost skin from the head of garlic. Cut off the very top of the head to expose the cloves. Place garlic in a small baking dish. Drizzle with the olive oil. Tuck a thyme sprig or two around the garlic. Bake, uncovered, for approximately 45 minutes or until garlic is tender. When cool enough to handle, break cloves off the bulb and squeeze roasted paste from individual cloves. It's that easy.

Nutrition information per serving, 8 servings per head: Calories: 13. Protein: 0g. Total fat: <1g (sat. fat: <1g). Carbohydrates: 2g. Cholesterol: 0mg. Sodium: 2mg. Vitamin A: 0%DV. Vitamin C: 3%DV.

This impressive spread is easy to make and yet so elegant—you're sure to get requests for the recipe. It is especially good spread on thin rice crackers.

Chèvre with Roasted Garlic

8 ounces chèvre (creamy goat cheese)
1 head roasted garlic
2 tablespoons minced fresh parsley
freshly ground black or white pepper to taste

Cream chèvre in a small bowl. Squeeze roasted garlic cloves into cheese and cream well. Stir in parsley and pepper. Mound cheese attractively on a plate or pack into small bowl. Chill for several hours or overnight. Garnish with fresh parsley sprigs. Serve with slices of French bread or thin, light crackers. For an extraordinary appetizer, spread chèvre on toasted baguette slices, top with a slice of garden fresh tomato, and embellish with a dollop of homemade pesto. This rich-tasting spread serves 10 to 12.

Nutrition information per serving, 10 servings per recipe: Calories: 69. Protein: 4g. Total fat: 4.8g (sat. fat: 3.6g). Carbohydrates: 1g. Cholesterol: 16mg. Sodium: 106mg. Vitamin A: 0% DV. Vitamin C: 3% DV.

NUTRITION INFORMATION PER 1 CLOVE GARLIC, RAW:

Calories: 4
Total fat: 0g
          (saturated fat: 0g)
Fiber: <1g
Sodium: 1mg
Potassium: <1% Daily Value
Vitamin A: 0% Daily Value
Vitamin C: 2% Daily Value
Iron: <1% Daily Value
Calcium: <1% Daily Value

GREEN BEANS

GREEN BEANS rank right up there with tomatoes, potatoes, and corn as a most popular and familiar vegetable. Green beans, or snap beans as they are more accurately called, can be grown on bushes or on vines that grow up on trellises or poles (yielding pole beans). Fresh snap beans from the garden, barely steamed, still bright green and full of fresh flavor, bear little resemblance to the dull, overcooked beans we ate from a can when I was growing up. In those days we called them "string beans" but that is really a misnomer since green beans have been stringless since 1894!

HANDLING: Truly fresh green beans should be crisp and will snap easily. They will keep for several days in the refrigerator stored loosely in a plastic bag—don't wash your green beans until you're ready to use them.

SIMPLE PREPARATION: Young snap beans can be prepared whole. Simply snap off the stem end, no need to trim the pointed end off. Most beans these days are the stringless variety and don't require removal of the string that used to run down the bean's side. Simple steaming for approximately 5 minutes is all a bean really needs. You can embellish further by tossing cooked beans around in a hot frying pan with a little melted butter, or add a splash of lemon juice and balsamic vinegar. Season with salt and pepper if you'd like. Larger beans should be snapped or cut before steaming and require additional time.

On a recent camping trip to Washington state, our family happened upon an organic farm stand near the entrance to North Cascades National Park. Besides incredible homemade ice cream and pints of beautiful blueberries, there were small bags of fresh-picked green beans that were truly a sight to behold. All slender, perfect, and uniform in size, packaged with the utmost care—I can picture them perfectly. They were a true feast—just the quality of bean you're looking for when you make Three Bean Salad.

Three Bean Salad

    2 to 3 cups lightly steamed green beans, cut into 1-inch pieces
    1½ cups cooked kidney beans
    1½ cups cooked garbanzo beans
    1 medium onion, cut into slivers
    1 green pepper, cut into slivers
    1 red pepper, cut into slivers
    5 tablespoons olive oil
    3 tablespoons balsamic vinegar*
    2 tablespoons sugar or honey
    chopped fresh basil to taste (dried may be substituted)
    chopped fresh parsley to taste
    ¼ teaspoon dried tarragon
    ¾ teaspoon salt
    black pepper to taste

Combine beans, onion and pepper slivers in a large bowl. Combine oil, vinegar, sweetener and herbs to make the dressing. Mix dressing well and toss with bean mixture. Season with salt and pepper. Refrigerate for several hours. Toss well before serving. Serves 8 as a side dish.

*Since balsamic vinegar is an aged red wine vinegar it has a very deep flavor. When using balsamic vinegar in recipes that call for cider vinegar or regular red wine vinegar you can usually use a smaller amount. In this recipe, if you want to use cider vinegar or regular wine vinegar, increase the amount of vinegar by 1 to 2 tablespoons.

Nutrition information per serving, 8 servings per recipe: Calories: 209 . Protein: 6g. Total fat: 8.7g (sat. fat: 1.2g). Carbohydrates: 25g. Cholesterol: 0mg. Sodium: 205mg. Vitamin A: 8% DV. Vitamin C: 60% DV.

Here is soup for the soul—thick and hearty with a little bit of kick from the black pepper. Make a pot of this soup when you need to turn a bad day around.

Marvelous Minestrone

2 tablespoons olive oil
4 to 6 cloves garlic, minced or pressed
1 large onion, chopped
2 medium carrots, chopped
4 to 5 stalks celery, chopped
2 tablespoons chopped fresh parsley
4 to 6 tablespoons fresh basil, chopped (or 2 teaspoons dried)
1 teaspoon dried oregano
1 teaspoon black pepper
1 teaspoon salt
3½ tablespoons red wine vinegar
2 tablespoons honey or brown sugar
5 to 7 cups water or stock (up to 1 cup red wine may be used as part of the liquid)
4 medium-sized fresh tomatoes, diced (or 1½ cups canned diced tomatoes)
1½ cups green beans, cut or snapped into 1-inch pieces
2 cups cooked kidney beans, rinsed and drained
8 ounces broken spaghetti, cooked

Heat olive oil in a large soup pot over medium heat. Add the garlic, onion, carrots, celery, parsley, basil, and oregano and sauté several minutes, until fragrant. Add pepper, salt, vinegar, sweetener, water or stock, tomatoes, and green beans. Bring to a boil, then reduce heat to low and simmer until vegetables are tender but not falling apart. Add the kidney beans and cooked pasta and heat through. If the soup is too thick at this point, add more water, stock, or red wine to thin it. Serve with freshly grated Parmesan or Asiago cheese, crusty French bread, and a crisp green salad—an excellent meal to share with friends. Serves 8.

Nutrition information per serving, 8 servings per recipe: Calories: 213. Protein: 7g. Total fat: 3.7g (sat. fat: <1g). Carbohydrates: 37g. Cholesterol: 0mg. Sodium: 297mg. Vitamin A: 55% DV. Vitamin C: 23% DV.

This comfortable and easy soup is perfect for a cool fall day. As it simmers, the kitchen will fill with the warm smell of cooking vegetables and barley, with a hint of cloves and thyme.

Simply Delicious Vegetable Barley Soup

⅓ cup pearled barley
6 to 7 cups water or vegetable stock
2 tablespoons canola oil
1 large onion, chopped
3 cloves garlic, minced or chopped
4 stalks celery, chopped
3 carrots, sliced
2 small zucchini (or other summer squash), chopped
1 large potato, chopped
1 cup green beans, cut in 1-inch pieces
1 bay leaf
1 to 2 cloves (wrapped in cheesecloth), or ¼ teaspoon ground cloves
1 teaspoon salt
½ teaspoon black pepper
pinch of crushed thyme

Put barley and water or stock in a soup pot. Bring to a boil over medium-high heat. Reduce heat to medium-low and simmer until barley is tender (approximately 1 hour). When barley is close to done, heat oil in a medium-sized skillet over medium heat. Add onions, garlic, and celery. Sauté until fragrant but not soft, approximately 5 to 8 minutes. Add these vegetables to barley and water, along with remaining ingredients. Increase heat to high and bring soup to a boil. Reduce heat to medium-low and cook until all vegetables are tender but not falling apart, approximately 20 to 25 minutes. If soup is too thick, add water to desired consistency. Serves 8.

Nutrition information per serving, 8 servings per recipe: Calories: 68. Protein: 1g. Total fat: 1.7g (sat. fat: <1g). Carbohydrates: 12g. Cholesterol: 0mg. Sodium: 304mg. Vitamin A: 97% DV. Vitamin C: 20% DV.

NUTRITION INFORMATION PER ½ CUP GREEN BEANS, RAW:

Calories: 22
Total fat: <0.2g
   (saturated fat: 0g)
Fiber: 2g
Sodium: 2mg
Potassium: 5% Daily Value
Vitamin A: 4% Daily Value
Vitamin C: 10% Daily Value
Iron: 4% Daily Value
Calcium: 3% Daily Value

GREEN BEANS

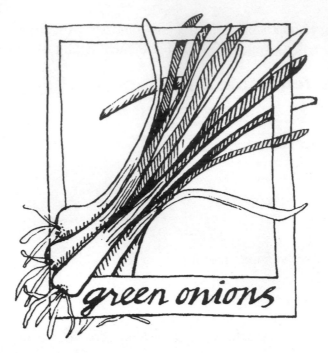

green onions

GREEN ONIONS

GREEN ONIONS are adolescent onions. They have a wonderful fresh and lively flavor. When you can get them locally grown they will often have little bits of dirt still clinging to their shallow roots—a testament to their freshness. Green onions are also known as scallions, which comes from *Ascalonia caepa,* or onion of Ascalon.

HANDLING: Green onions are rather undemanding. They store well in a plastic bag in the refrigerator for about a week. Don't wash them until you're ready to use them.

SIMPLE PREPARATION: Rinse green onions under cool running water. Trim off the root end and remove the outermost skin. Chopped raw green onions are excellent in salads, as a taco topping, and as a beautiful and tasty embellishment in a bowl of delicate noodle soup. Green onions are also perfect in stir-fry.

Here's just the right dish to make when you're really too tired to cook. It's quick and easy and very comforting. It is also surprisingly good cold for lunch the next day.

Cheesey Orzo with Carrots and Green Onions

1 cup uncooked orzo (rice shaped pasta)
2 carrots, cut into matchstick pieces
12 ounces lowfat cottage cheese
½ cup plain yogurt or light sour cream
4 green onions, minced
2 tablespoons chopped fresh parsley
½ teaspoon salt
freshly ground black pepper to taste

Cook orzo and carrots in boiling water until orzo is just tender, approximately 10 to 12 minutes. Drain thoroughly. While pasta is still hot, toss with cottage cheese, yogurt or sour cream, green onions, parsley, salt, and pepper. Serve immediately. Serves 6.

Nutrition information per serving, 6 servings per recipe: Calories: 102. Protein: 10g. Total fat: <1g (sat. fat: <1g). Carbohydrates: 13g. Cholesterol: 3.8mg. Sodium: 412mg. Vitamin A: 73% DV. Vitamin C: 14% DV.

Potato pancakes are great for a leisurely weekend breakfast or anytime for a quick dinner idea. Serve them with homemade applesauce.

Green Onion and Potato Pancakes

   1 pound of potatoes (3 to 4 medium potatoes)
   1 teaspoon olive oil
   12 green onions, bulbs and greens, chopped
   ¼ cup minced parsley
   ½ cup fresh bread crumbs
   2 eggs, beaten
   ½ cup lowfat sour cream
   1 teaspoon salt
   lots of freshly ground black pepper
   2 to 3 tablespoons oil for frying

Wash potatoes, cut into big chunks, boil, and mash—no need to peel, the skins add nice texture and color to the pancakes. Heat olive oil in a small skillet over medium heat. Add green onions and sauté for 3 minutes, until just tender. Combine potatoes, onions, and remaining ingredients, except for frying oil. Stir well. Heat 1 tablespoon of the frying oil in a large skillet over medium heat. Drop pancake mixture onto hot skillet, approximately 2 heaping tablespoons per pancake. Flatten with a spatula. Fry 2 to 3 minutes on each side until golden brown. Repeat for rest of mixture. Makes 12 to 14 pancakes.

Nutrition information per pancake: Calories: 104. Protein: 2.5g. Total fat: 5.2g (sat. fat: 1.6g). Carbohydrates: 12g. Cholesterol: 31mg. Sodium: 230mg. Vitamin A: 11% DV. Vitamin C: 20% DV.

This delicate soup can be made in no time at all. It is full of the fresh flavors of spring with bright-tasting green onions and crunchy snow peas. For best results use a flavorful homemade vegetable broth for the base.

Spring Soup

1 tablespoon sesame oil
2 cups chopped green onions
1 teaspoon grated fresh ginger root
2 tablespoons reduced-sodium soy sauce
6 to 7 cups water or vegetable broth (up to ½ cup of this can be dry white wine)
several generous grinds black pepper
1 cup snow peas, sliced in half, on the diagonal
½ to ¾ cup cooked basmati rice (optional)
¼ to ⅓ cup chopped green onions for garnish

Heat oil in a soup pot over medium heat. Add green onions and ginger. Sauté for 2 to 3 minutes. Add soy sauce, water or broth, and black pepper. Simmer for 2 to 3 minutes. Add snow peas. Simmer 1 to 2 more minutes. Serve immediately. A tablespoon or two of cooked white or brown basmati rice may be added to each serving if desired. Garnish with raw, chopped green onion. Serves 6.

Nutrition information per serving, 6 servings per recipe: Calories: 39. Protein: 1g. Total fat: 2.2g (sat. fat: <1g). Carbohydrates: 3g. Cholesterol: 0mg. Sodium: 201mg. Vitamin A: 16% DV. Vitamin C: 51% DV.

NUTRITION INFORMATION PER 1 GREEN ONION, RAW:

Calories: 2
Total fat: 0g
    (saturated fat: 0g)
Fiber: 0.5g
Sodium: 0mg
Potassium: 1% Daily Value
Vitamin A: 7% Daily Value
Vitamin C: 12% Daily Value
Iron: 1% Daily Value
Calcium: <1% Daily Value

green onions

ARUGULA AND MIZUNA are not everyday fare in most kitchens,

but that is slowly changing. Arugula, also known as Rocket, is a tender, slightly bitter or peppery green popular in the Mediterrancan. Arugula has small, flat leaves on long stems and somewhat resembles dandelion greens. Arugula adds enough flavor to a dish to almost be an herb and has been referred to in old herbals as "a seasoning leaf". It definitely has a more sophisticated taste than mild-mannered greens such as kale or chard. Mizuna, also called Japanese mustard green, has a distinctive personality. Its more feathery leaves offer a mild mustard flavor and it is often incorporated into mesclun, a mix of baby salad greens.

HANDLING: Small greens such as arugula and mizuna are very perishable. They are best used a day or two after buying them. Wrap a damp towel around the root ends and store in a loose plastic bag in the refrigerator. Trim the root ends off and wash the greens well in cool water just before you're ready to use them in a salad or a cooked dish. You may have to wash them several times to remove sand and dirt. Be diligent about this—nothing ruins a salad faster than the crunch of sand or grit. If you'll be using arugula or mizuna in a salad, you can spin the leaves dry in a salad spinner.

SIMPLE PREPARATION: Both of these greens add dimension to simple green salad. There is no easier way to enjoy their flavorful personality than tossed with a selection of mild greens, dressed with a sharp vinaigrette, and topped with homemade croutons. A single arugula leaf can turn a simple sandwich into elegant picnic food. Spread baguette slices or focaccia with goat cheese, roasted red pepper, and top with arugula. Both arugula and mizuna can be lightly steamed or stir-fried and tossed with cooked pasta or potatoes.

Very fresh greens are a must for this delicious dish. It is really excellent made with a mixture of mizuna and baby spinach with a little arugula added in for flavor. The tofu should be fresh (not the silken variety) and firm.

Mizuna with Minced Tofu

3 cloves garlic, pressed or minced
1 teaspoon finely grated fresh ginger
2 teaspoons soy sauce
4 teaspoons peanut oil
1 pound tofu, minced
1 carrot, diced
1 small onion, minced
⅓ cup minced water chestnuts
juice of 1 lemon
½ teaspoon chili paste (optional)
approximately 1 pound mizuna (or a combination of mizuna, baby spinach, and arugula)
½ teaspoon salt
freshly ground black pepper

For the marinade, combine garlic, ginger, soy sauce, and 2 teaspoons peanut oil in a medium-sized bowl. Add minced tofu and toss until tofu has absorbed marinade. Set aside for 30 minutes. Heat 1 teaspoon peanut oil in a wok or large skillet over medium heat. Add tofu plus marinade and sauté for 10 minutes, stirring frequently to prevent sticking. Remove from pan and set aside. Heat remaining 1 teaspoon oil in wok or skillet over medium heat and add the carrots, onions, and water chestnuts. Sauté for 3 to 4 minutes. Add lemon juice and chili paste, then the mizuna. Stir until mizuna wilts slightly. Add tofu and toss. Season with salt and plenty of black pepper. Serve mounded on top of basmati rice. Serves 4.

Nutrition information per serving, 4 servings per recipe: Calories: 151. Protein: 10g. Total fat: 6.8g (sat. fat: 1g). Carbohydrates: 11g. Cholesterol: 0mg. Sodium: 500mg. Vitamin A: 90% DV. Vitamin C: 48% DV.

About the time arugula is in season in Kansas, we are also fortunate to have fresh shiitake mushrooms grown by friends Alan and Mary Terry of Baldwin, Kansas. Here is a recipe that combines these two very distinctive ingredients, punctuated by salty Kalamata olives and the slight heat of chili flakes—not a subtle dish, but most definitely sure to please those fond of heartier pasta dishes.

Pasta with Arugula, Kalamata Olives, and Shiitake Mushrooms

¾ pound penne pasta
1½ tablespoons olive oil
1 to 3 cloves garlic, minced or pressed
2 ounces fresh shiitake mushrooms, chopped
2 pounds fresh roma tomatoes, peeled and chopped
¼ teaspoon or more dried red chili flakes
5 tablespoons chopped Kalamata olives
½ teaspoon salt
1½ cups chopped arugula
½ cup freshly grated Parmesan or Asiago cheese

Put on a large pot of water and cook the pasta while you prepare the sauce. Heat the olive oil in a large, deep skillet over medium heat. Add the garlic and mushrooms and sauté for 2 to 3 minutes. Add the tomatoes, chili flakes, olives, and salt. Allow the sauce to simmer approximately 10 minutes. By now your pasta should be cooked. Drain it well and toss with the chopped arugula. Heap pasta in a large bowl, pour on the sauce and toss lightly again. Top with grated cheese and serve immediately. Serves 4.

Nutrition information per serving, 4 servings per recipe: Calories: 413. Protein: 14g. Total fat: 12g (sat. fat: 3.3g). Carbohydrates: 60g. Cholesterol: 8mg. Sodium: 618mg. Vitamin A: 34% DV. Vitamin C: 77% DV.

Here is a most basic salad with a simple vinaigrette. It is important to use only the freshest garden tomatoes. Be creative and add strips of golden bell pepper, slivers of fresh basil, or crumbles of Feta cheese.

Simple Salad of Arugula, Red Onions, and Garden Tomatoes

1 to 2 bunches arugula (about 1 handful of leaves per person)
½ small red onion, cut into very thin slices
approximately 1 pound fresh garden tomatoes chopped in large pieces (an assortment of colors and varieties is especially nice)

Dressing:
2 tablespoons olive oil
2 teaspoons balsamic vinegar
½ of a small shallot, minced
¼ teaspoon salt
freshly ground black pepper to taste

Wash the arugula, spin or pat dry. Remove tough stems. Place in a large, shallow salad bowl. Arrange onion rings and chopped tomatoes on top of arugula leaves. Whisk or shake the dressing ingredients together. Dress and toss salad at the dinner table. Serve immediately. Serves 4.

Nutrition information per serving, 4 servings per recipe: Calories: 97.5. Protein: 1g. Total fat: 6.5g (sat. fat: <1g). Carbohydrates: 7g. Cholesterol: 0mg. Sodium: 147mg. Vitamin A: 27% DV. Vitamin C: 60% DV.

NUTRITION INFORMATION PER 1 CUP RAW ARUGULA:

Calories: 13
Total fat: 0g
   (saturated fat: 0g)
Fiber: Not available
Sodium: 0mg
Potassium: Not available
Vitamin A: Not available
Vitamin C: 75% Daily Value
Iron: 3% Daily Value
Calcium: 16% Daily Value

MIZUNA

KALE

COLLARDS AND KALE (as well as Swiss chard and mustard greens)
are solid, dependable, nutritious vegetables that are often overlooked and underrated. They lack
the sophistication of greens like arugula and mizuna. They lack the familiarity and comfort of
vegetables like green beans, corn, and tomatoes. They're humble . . . and so very delicious . . .
and each unique. For the most part they are interchangeable in many recipes, although I must
say I definitely have my prejudice. Pass the kale please.

HANDLING: Really fresh greens will hold for up to a week in the refrigerator. Bag greens
loosely in plastic and don't wash them until you're ready to use them. Thick, hardy kale leaves
are less prone to bruising and will usually last longer than more tender chard. Make sure your
greens are fresh, with no yellow tinge, or they'll deteriorate quickly.

SIMPLE PREPARATION: Wash greens thoroughly—their curly, textured leaves often hold dirt.
If the greens are large and mature you'll need to cut the leaves from the large stems. Younger
greens can be cut up, stem and all. At our house we sauté greens lightly in a little bit of olive oil
with a bit of minced garlic. There is usually just enough water clinging to the leaves from
washing to help steam the greens. Add a splash of soy sauce during cooking. Cook greens until
they are just tender but still colorful and alive. Mustard greens and collards have a slightly
stronger flavor than chard or kale and may benefit from slower cooking in soups or broths to
help mellow their sharpness.

Quiches have a reputation for being time-consuming to prepare. If you skip the crust and bake your quiche directly in a baking dish, they are really easy and quick to make. This recipe uses mostly whole eggs. We use fresh, local eggs which have great taste and color. If you prefer, egg whites can be substituted to reduce fat and cholesterol.

Kansas Quiche

1 pound chopped chard, yellow summer squash, zucchini, or a combination
½ onion, chopped
3 whole eggs
1 egg white
½ cup skim or lowfat milk
1½ cups grated Swiss cheese
½ teaspoon salt
¼ teaspoon pepper
½ teaspoon dried basil
¼ teaspoon dried oregano

Steam chard, squash, or a combination with onions until tender. Set aside to cool slightly. Preheat oven to 375°F. Beat eggs thoroughly. Add milk, grated cheese, salt, pepper, and herbs. Blend in steamed vegetables and mix together well. Pour into medium-sized oiled casserole dish and bake, covered, until set—approximately 30 to 40 minutes. Serves 4.

Nutrition information per serving, 4 servings per recipe: Calories: 184. Protein: 15g. Total fat: 10.2g (sat. fat: 5.7g). Carbohydrates: 7g. Cholesterol: 145mg. Sodium: 583mg. Vitamin A: 56% DV. Vitamin C: 56% DV.

For the last two years, a group of women in Lawrence, Kansas has organized a day-long conference focused on health care options for women. This year, on the day of the conference, we arranged to have the deli at Community Mercantile feed our speakers and hard-working taskforce. Good friend Laurie Ward drove to the co-op and brought back a steaming hot pan of vegetable lasagna. We were nourished by this delicious comfort food.

Summer Lasagna

1 tablespoon olive oil
2 to 4 cloves garlic, minced or pressed
1 medium onion, chopped
2 small zucchini or other summer squash, chopped
1 teaspoon dried basil
1 quart pasta sauce (homemade or prepared)
9 lasagna noodles (approximately ½ pound)
1 bunch Swiss chard
1½ cups lowfat cottage or Ricotta cheese
1 beaten egg white
¼ teaspoon salt
freshly ground black pepper
½ pound Mozzarella, grated
½ cup grated Parmesan

Heat oil in large saucepan or deep skillet over medium heat and sauté garlic, onion, and zucchini until just barely tender. Stir in basil and pasta sauce and allow to simmer over low heat while you prepare the rest of the lasagna. Cook lasagna noodles in boiling water until just barely tender. Drain and rinse with cold water (I like to lay my cooked noodles out on the counter so they won't stick together). Wash chard well, trim the tough stems, and steam or boil whole leaves until they are just tender. Drain leaves well, squeeze out excess water, and chop. Mix cottage or Ricotta cheese and egg white together thoroughly. Season with salt and pepper. Blend in chard. Now you're ready to assemble—the fun part! Preheat oven to 350°F. Place ¼ cup of the sauce in the bottom of a 9 x 13-inch baking pan. Line the bottom of the pan with 3 of the cooked lasagna noodles. Spread half of the cottage or Ricotta cheese mixture on top of the noodles. Cover this with half of the Mozzarella. Top this with a third of the sauce, spreading as evenly as possible. Repeat with three more noodles, the remaining cottage or Ricotta cheese, the remaining Mozzarella, approximately half of the sauce you have left, and cover all this with the last 3 noodles. You should have just enough sauce to cover the top of the noodles. Sprinkle with the Parmesan. Cover pan with foil and bake for 40 minutes. Remove foil and bake another 10 to 15 minutes, uncovered. Remove from oven and allow to sit several minutes before serving. Serves 8.

Nutrition information per serving, 8 servings per recipe: Calories: 323. Protein: 22g. Total fat: 10g (sat. fat: 5.4g). Carbohydrates: 35g. Cholesterol: 30mg. Sodium: 514mg. Vitamin A: 69% DV. Vitamin C: 24% DV.

NUTRITION INFORMATION PER ½ CUP, COOKED:

COLLARDS:
Calories: 18
Total fat: <0.2g
    (saturated fat: 0g)
Fiber: 1.8g
Sodium: 18mg
Potassium: 3% Daily Value
Vitamin A: 21% Daily Value
Vitamin C: 15% Daily Value
Iron: 2% Daily Value
Calcium: 7% Daily Value

KALE:
Calories: 21
Total fat: <0.2g
    (saturated fat: <.1g)
Fiber: 1.7g
Sodium: 15mg
Potassium: 4% Daily Value
Vitamin A: 48% Daily Value
Vitamin C: 45% Daily Value
Iron: 3% Daily Value
Calcium: 5% Daily Value

SWISS CHARD:
Calories: 13
Total fat: 0g
    (saturated fat: 0g)
Fiber: 3.7g
Sodium: 158mg
Potassium: 14% Daily Value
Vitamin A: 28% Daily Value
Vitamin C: 27% Daily Value
Iron: 11% Daily Value
Calcium: 5% Daily Value

MUSTARD:
Calories: 21
Total fat: 0
    (saturated fat: 0g)
Fiber: 1.3g
Sodium: 11mg
Potassium: 4% Daily Value
Vitamin A: 21% Daily Value
Vitamin C: 30% Daily Value
Iron: 3% Daily Value
Calcium: 5% Daily Value

KOHLRABI

KOHLRABI can be one of those intimidating vegetables if you haven't been around it much. It has the look of an organic green Sputnik, with a taste like fresh, crunchy broccoli stems accented by radish. The name kohlrabi comes from the German *kohl,* meaning cabbage, and *rabi,* or turnip, and that kind of sums it up. Although these green bulbs look like they were dug up from the earth, the round bulb is a swollen stem that grows aboveground. Not a commonly used vegetable in American cuisine, kohlrabi is widely used in Central Europe and Asia. It is still patiently waiting to be discovered in this country.

HANDLING: If the kohlrabi leaves are still attached to the bulb, trim them and store separately. If the leaves are in good shape—firm and green—they can be cooked but will need to be used within a couple of days. The bulbs should be stored, unwashed, in a plastic bag. They will hold for about a week in the refrigerator. Smaller kohlrabi are the sweetest and most tender. Bulbs much bigger than the size of a tennis ball won't be as tasty and often have a pithy flesh.

SIMPLE PREPARATION: Tender, young kohlrabi is delicious eaten raw. Peel the outer skin with a paring knife. Slice, dice, or grate, and add to salads. Use on raw vegetable platters or serve with a creamy dip. Substitute in recipes calling for radishes. Grated kohlrabi can be added to slaw, but lightly salt it first and let stand for several minutes. Squeeze to remove any excess water before adding dressing. Kohlrabi can also be steamed or boiled. For this preparation, don't peel until after they are cooked. Steam or boil until bulbs are tender, peel skin, and season with butter, salt, and pepper, a cheese sauce, or just enjoy plain. Try sautéeing grated kohlrabi. Peel the bulbs and coarsely grate. Heat a small amount of olive oil in a skillet, add kohlrabi and sauté until tender-crisp. Season with salt and pepper, or add a snip of fresh dill weed or oregano. If the leaves attached to the kohlrabi bulb are fresh and green, they can be enjoyed as a cooked green. Wash the leaves and remove the ribs. Blanch in boiling water until just wilted, 3 to 5 minutes. Drain and squeeze excess water from leaves. Chop leaves, then sauté in a little olive oil or butter. Season with salt and pepper. Add a splash of vinegar or squeeze of fresh lemon juice.

Here's a quick pasta recipe that combines kohlrabi with light summer vegetables and a hint of fresh thyme—really delicious, and sweet when prepared with fresh kohlrabi.

Rotini Pasta with Kohlrabi

½ pound rotini pasta (or other spiral shape)
2 tablespoons olive oil
2 cloves garlic, minced or pressed
1 small onion, cut in slivers
3 or 4 small kohlrabi bulbs, coarsely shredded
1 large carrot, coarsely shredded
1 large bell pepper, chopped (red, yellow, or green)
the leaves from 1 sprig of fresh thyme
½ teaspoon salt
freshly ground black pepper
freshly grated Parmesan or Asiago cheese

Put on a large pot of water and boil the pasta while you prepare the vegetables. Heat olive oil in a large, heavy skillet over medium heat. Sauté the garlic and onions for 2 to 3 minutes. Add the kohlrabi, carrot, bell pepper, thyme leaves, salt, and black pepper. Continue cooking, stirring often, until all vegetables are just barely tender-crisp. If vegetables begin to stick add several tablespoons of water to the skillet. Drain the cooked pasta and place hot pasta in a large, shallow bowl. Heap cooked vegetables on top of pasta.Sprinkle with Parmesan or Asiago and garnish with sprigs of fresh thyme. Serves 6.

Nutrition information per serving, 6 servings per recipe: Calories: 170. Protein: 4g. Total fat: 4.6g (sat. fat: <1g). Carbohydrates: 27g. Cholesterol: 0mg. Sodium: 193mg. Vitamin A: 35% DV. Vitamin C: 79% DV.

When the weather is cool and your tastes turn to warm comforting foods, try this earthy stew. Serve in bowls over a scoop of brown rice with thick slices of dark bread to dunk into the broth.

Fall Stew with Kohlrabi

    2 or 3 medium-sized kohlrabi, bulbs and greens
    1 tablespoon olive oil
    1 large onion, cut in slivers
    3 medium carrots, cut into ¾-inch chunks
    2 medium potatoes, cut into ¾-inch chunks
    1 cup peeled, chopped tomatoes (Italian-style tomatoes are particularly good)
    4 cups vegetable broth
    1 bay leaf
    ½ teaspoon dried oregano
    1 teaspoon salt
    freshly ground black pepper to taste
    1 tablespoon Dijon mustard
    ½ tablespoon molasses

Separate leaves from kohlrabi bulbs. Peel bulbs and cut into large chunks. Derib leaves and cut into thin strips. Set aside. Heat oil in a large soup pot over medium heat. Add onions and sauté for several minutes. Add kohlrabi bulb chunks, carrots, potatoes, tomatoes, broth, bay leaf, oregano, salt, black pepper, molasses, and mustard. Turn heat up to medium-high and bring stew to a boil. Reduce heat to medium-low, cover, and simmer stew for approximately 15 minutes or until vegetables are not quite tender. Add kohlrabi leaves and simmer, uncovered for another 10 minutes or until vegetables are just cooked. Serves 6.

Nutrition information per serving, 6 servings per recipe: Calories: 185. Protein: 6g. Total fat: 2.1g (sat. fat: <1g). Carbohydrates: 32 g. Cholesterol: 0mg. Sodium: 518mg. Vitamin A: 95% DV. Vitamin C: 97% DV.

NUTRITION INFORMATION PER ½ CUP KOHLRABI, RAW:

    Calories:19
    Total fat: 0g
          (saturated fat: 0g)
    Fiber: 1.5g
    Sodium: 14mg
    Potassium: 7% Daily Value
    Vitamin A: <1% Daily Value
    Vitamin C: 72% Daily Value
    Iron: 2% Daily Value
    Calcium: 2% Daily Value

KOHLRABI

LEEKS

LEEKS

LEEKS are subtle and buttery and well worth the effort of washing them. A member of the onion family, leeks have a more refined and delicate taste than regular onions. They are a staple in Europe, where they are commonly used in soups, stews, and main dishes. Leeks have a well-deserved reputation for harboring dirt—it is often true that the broad, flat leaves catch and hold sand and soil. But this is a small challenge and once you've made a pot of Potato Leek Soup you'll be happy to carefully bathe these onion cousins. In Wales, leeks serve a nonculinary use as hat decorations on St. David's Day. This is a time when Britons celebrate their heroic resistance to the Saxon invasion in the sixth century A.D. Legend has it that the people of Wales were directed by St. David to wear leeks in their hats to distinguish themselves from the enemy. It has potential.

HANDLING: Leeks keep well in the refrigerator. Place them unwashed, roots still attached, in a plastic bag, but don't seal. Make sure the leeks are dry when stored—if they are trapped in a bag with moisture they won't keep well. Careful washing is the first order when you're ready to cook your leeks. Trim the dark green leaves down to where they just begin to turn pale. Trim the roots. Remove the very outer leaves. Slit the leek lengthwise almost to the core. Fan out the leaves and rinse well under running water.

SIMPLE PREPARATION: After thorough cleaning, chop or slice leeks and use in much the same way you would use onions. Leeks develop the best flavor with slow cooking or sautéeing. They can also be eaten whole, either steamed or boiled. After trimming and washing, cook until tender and serve with a light cream or tomato sauce. Baby leeks can be steamed and served with lemon butter, to be eaten like asparagus.

Potato Leek Soup is a classic. You can find variations on it almost everywhere cooks write about potatoes and leeks. This version has a light, delicate taste with a touch of thyme.

Potato Leek Soup

2 tablespoons butter
2 cups sliced leeks
3 stalks celery, chopped
6 cups chopped potatoes*
6 cups vegetable stock
2 tablespoons fresh lemon juice
¼ cup chopped fresh parsley
1 sprig fresh thyme (or ½ teaspoon dried)
¾ teaspoon salt
1 cup lowfat milk
freshly ground black pepper
sour cream or yogurt and minced fresh parsley for garnish

Heat the butter in a large soup pot over medium-low heat. Add leeks and celery and sauté until tender. Add potatoes, stock, lemon juice, parsley, thyme, and salt. Increase heat and bring to a boil. Reduce heat to medium-low and simmer until potatoes are tender, approximately 15 to 20 minutes. If you're using fresh thyme, remove the sprig. Remove half the soup from the pot and allow to cool slightly. Put this soup in a blender and whir it up until smooth and creamy. Return soup to the pot. Very slowly, stir in the milk. Heat through over low heat. Season with black pepper to taste. Serve garnished with a dollop of sour cream or yogurt and a sprinkling of minced parsley. Serves 6.

*Whether or not you peel the potatoes is a matter of preference. For most recipes, I don't even think about peeling. I like the look, taste, and texture of potato peels. In this soup I can go either way. Peeling the potatoes makes a milky white, very smooth and delicate soup. Leaving the peels on adds little flecks and pieces of skin for a slightly heartier effect.

Nutrition information per serving, 6 servings per recipe: Calories: 249. Protein: 8g Total fat: 3.8g (sat. fat: 2.4g). Carbohydrates: 45g. Cholesterol: 11mg. Sodium: 519mg. Vitamin A: 40% DV. Vitamin C: 45% DV.

Here is a lovely and versatile topping that can be used for pizza, tossed with hot pasta, or mixed with Ricotta to create a very special lasagna filling.

Leek and Dried Tomato Topping

⅓ cup dried tomatoes
1 tablespoon olive oil
2 garlic cloves, pressed or minced
3 medium leeks, thinly sliced
1 tablespoon red wine or water
¼ cup coarsely chopped fresh basil
½ teaspoon salt
freshly ground black pepper to taste

Place dried tomatoes in a small bowl and cover with boiling water. Let stand 10 to 15 minutes. Drain off the water and chop tomatoes. Set aside. Heat oil in a medium-sized skillet over medium heat. Add garlic and leeks. Sauté, stirring frequently, for 5 minutes. Add the wine or water, and the chopped tomatoes. Cook for 5 more minutes or until leeks are tender. Remove from heat. Toss in the basil and sprinkle with salt and pepper. For a wonderfully flavorful pizza, spread topping directly on crust, top with smoked Provolone and freshly grated Parmesan. Bake until golden. For even more flavor add sautéed strips of fresh shiitake to the pizza before covering with cheese. As a pasta topping, simply toss with hot cooked pasta of your choice. Grate on plenty of Parmesan or Asiago cheese. For a special lasagna filling, mix topping in with Ricotta. Serves 4.

Nutrition information per serving, 4 servings per recipe: Calories: 136. Protein: 2g. Total fat: 3.3g (sat. fat: 0.4g). Carbohydrates: 16g. Cholesterol: 0mg. Sodium: 323mg. Vitamin A: 1% DV. Vitamin C: 20% DV.

NUTRITION INFORMATION PER ¼ CUP LEEKS, RAW:

Calories: 16
Total fat: 0g
   (saturated fat: 0g)
Fiber: .8g
Sodium: 5mg
Potassium: 1% Daily Value
Vitamin A: <1% Daily Value
Vitamin C: 5% Daily Value
Iron: 3% Daily Value
Calcium: 2% Daily Value

LEEKS

LETTUCE

LETTUCE, as I knew it growing up, meant iceberg lettuce. Its durable, crispy leaves provided a perfect vehicle for salad dressing. Crisp head lettuces, such as iceberg, are still the mainstay on many salad bars, but other more interesting and nutritious lettuces are now widely available. Butterheads, or bibbs, are soft and delicate lettuces that grow in a rosette formation. Loose leafs are more open with foliage that is ruffled or sometimes deeply indented. Cos or romaine lettuces have long, crisp leaves with a heart of milder flavored, blanched leaves. Many of these lettuces appear in greens and "reds" (really more bronze or deep burgundy). Salad mix, also called mesclun from the French word *mesclumo,* meaning "a mixture", provides a contrast of tastes, textures, and colors from a variety of baby greens and herbs.

HANDLING: Keep lettuce loosely stored in a plastic bag in the refrigerator. Don't wash it until you are ready to use. Salad mix often comes in its own bag, which couldn't be easier. When choosing salad mix take a close look before you buy. Make sure the greens are fresh (a very good reason to buy locally grown salad mix). Those little baby leaves are extremely delicate, and if they are at all damaged the taste of the whole mix will be negatively affected.

SIMPLE PREPARATION: To prepare leaf or head lettuce for salad, wash carefully in a sink of cool water. Be sure to dry your lettuce thoroughly before arranging your salad—nothing is worse than waterlogged greens with diluted salad dressing. Salad spinners do an excellent job and are a fairly inexpensive, low-technology solution for drying greens. Salad mixes are usually clean enough to eat right out of the bag. Take the time to carefully sort and remove damaged leaves before serving. When you are ready to compose your salad, rip the larger leaves into manageable-sized pieces, discarding the thicker stems and damaged leaves. Enjoy arranging the leaves in a large bowl or on a platter. Dress the whole salad only if you think it will be eaten at that meal—salad with dressing doesn't keep. And a word here about salad dressings. Bottled dressings are convenient, but they are often heavy and can't compare with the fresh, light taste of a simple, homemade vinaigrette (like the following dressing for Classic Greek Salad).

The fun part about serving a Greek salad, or any salad for that matter, is putting it together. Prepare all your vegetables, get out a large platter or favorite salad bowl, and begin construction. A salad that is put together with care and patience can become the centerpiece of a meal.

Classic Greek Salad

1 medium head romaine lettuce, torn in bite-sized pieces
1 cup torn radicchio* (if available)
1 pound tomatoes (ideally an assortment of colors and varieties), cut into wedges. Halve cherry tomatoes and small plum tomatoes.
1 small cucumber (preferably the thin variety), cut in thin slices
¼ red onion, thinly sliced
12 Kalamata olives
2 ounces crumbled Feta cheese
8 to 10 fresh basil leaves, cut in thin ribbons

Toss lettuce and radicchio together and heap on a platter or in a large salad bowl. Arrange remaining vegetables on top of lettuce in order given, ending with the ribbons of fresh basil which will be scattered over the top of your salad. Just before serving, dress your salad with the following vinaigrette.

Dressing:
3 tablespoons olive oil
2 tablespoons white wine vinegar
1 tablespoon minced fresh oregano (or 1 teaspoon dried oregano)
1 clove garlic, minced
¼ teaspoon salt
freshly ground black pepper

Combine dressing ingredients in a small bowl and whisk together. Salad with dressing serves 4.

*Radicchio, also known as Red Chicory, is a beautifully colored, slightly bitter green that will add a little bite and a lovely touch of magenta to this salad. It is not necessary—just a little something special.

Nutrition information per serving, 4 servings per recipe: Calories: 188. Protein: 3g. Total fat: 14.1g (sat. fat: 3.6g). Carbohydrates: 9g. Cholesterol: 12.5mg. Sodium: 618mg. Vitamin A: 28% DV. Vitamin C: 53% DV.

Oranges and red onions combine with fennel to create an elegant green salad.

Salad with Oranges, Fennel, and Fresh Basil

1 head looseleaf lettuce, torn into bite-sized pieces
2 seedless oranges, peeled and cut into thin slices which are then cut in half
¼ cup thinly sliced red onion
slivers of fennel bulb (to taste)
2 cups homemade croutons
ribbons of fresh basil leaves (to taste)

Heap lettuce on platter or in shallow salad bowl. Arrange orange slices, red onion, and fennel slivers on top of lettuce. Scatter croutons and fresh basil on top. Dress right before serving.

Dressing:
4 tablespoons olive oil
1½ tablespoons balsamic or red wine vinegar
¼ teaspoon salt
freshly ground black pepper

Combine dressing ingredients in a small bowl and whisk together. Salad with dressing serves 4.

Nutrition information per serving, 4 servings per recipe: Calories: 156. Protein: 2g. Total fat: 10.5g (sat. fat: 2.6g). Carbohydrates: 12g. Cholesterol: 1.3mg. Sodium: 234mg. Vitamin A: 3% DV. Vitamin C: 44% DV.

Homemade Croutons are a simple affair, but you need good bread to start with. Day-old baguettes, or chewy Italian bread that's slightly dried out are both excellent choices. Preheat oven to 400°F. Cut bread into small cubes. Place on a baking sheet that has been brushed with olive oil. Bake until just crunchy, turning once or twice. How long the croutons take will depend on the bread you're using and the size of your cubes. Keep a watchful eye—they can quickly turn too brown. For extra flavor, croutons can be tossed with just enough olive oil to hold freshly minced herbs in place. You can also rub garlic on the bread slices before they are cubed.

NUTRITION INFORMATION PER ½ CUP LOOSE-LEAF LETTUCE, RAW:

Calories: 5
Total fat: 0g
   (saturated fat: 0g)
Fiber: 0.4g
Sodium: 3mg
Potassium: 2% Daily Value
Vitamin A: 5% Daily Value
Vitamin C: 8% Daily Value
Iron: 2% Daily Value
Calcium: 2% Daily Value

ONIONS

ONIONS are a mainstay in most modern-day kitchens, following a long, long history of popularity and usage. Onions originated in prehistoric times and have been eaten raw and cooked in one of their over 500 manifestations by almost all cultures. We've discussed leeks and scallions separately—the species of *Allium* we're discussing here are the most familiar bulb onions, like golden-skinned Spanish onions, and fresh-from-the-ground sweet onions like Vidalias. Storage-type onions have dry, crackly outer skins, are harvested later in the growing season, and are cured to store well. Sweet onions have a more tender outer skin and generally have a milder taste. Sweet onions should be used soon after their harvest—they are not intended for storage. And why do onions make you blue? Chopping onions releases volatile compounds that irritate the eyes. It seems the older an onion is, the stronger the compounds. Cooking causes chemical alterations to these irritating compounds, making them much milder.

HANDLING: Regular Spanish-type onions should be completely dry for optimal storage. They will keep best if they have some air circulation and cool, dry conditions. If onions are stored in a warm and humid place in your kitchen they will more quickly sprout. Sweet onions should be stored in the refrigerator and used soon after harvest.

SIMPLE PREPARATION: For sweet onions, trim off the green tops as well as the root end. Chop or slice as you would a storage onion. The only noticeable difference will be that the sweet onion is more juicy. Use in cooking as you would any onion. You will enjoy the nice mild character of sweet onions. For storage onions, slice off both ends of the onion. Slit the outer skin the length of the bulb and slip it off. Exactly how you slice, chop, or mince the onion will be determined by your recipe, but one important piece of equipment is necessary to do a good job—a very sharp knife. If there is just one kitchen item you invest in, let it be an excellent knife. Good knives are expensive. Some of the best are made in Germany and you can easily spend over $100 on a large chef's knife. Once you use a high quality knife you will wonder how you got by without it. If you take care of your knife, you will never need to make this purchase again.

Equally good for brunch or dinner, serve slices of this crustless quiche with thick slices of fresh tomatoes, wedges of ripe melon, and wholegrain rolls.

Savory Onion Potato Pie

    1 tablespoon butter
    2 medium-sized onions, chopped coarsely
    3 eggs
    ¾ cup skim milk
    3 to 4 medium-sized potatoes, unpeeled, cooked, cubed
    3½ ounces Gruyere or other Swiss cheese, grated
    ½ teaspoon salt
    black pepper to taste
    a sprinkle of grated nutmeg

Melt butter in a heavy skillet over medium heat. Add onions and sauté, stirring often, until slightly browned, but not quite transparent, approximately 10 to 15 minutes. Remove from heat and allow to cool slightly. Beat eggs and milk together. Stir in cooked potatoes, grated cheese, salt, pepper, and nutmeg. Pour into a deep 9½ inch pie plate and bake for 30 minutes, or until beautifully golden on top and fully set. Serves 6.

Variations: For a really deep and full flavor, substitute smoked provolone for all or part of the Swiss cheese. For a special occasion, bake filling in a pie crust.. This, of course, adds extra work (and fat!) so you wouldn't want to do it all the time. But for company dinner or a birthday feast this simple onion pie will be transformed into an elegant quiche.

Nutrition information per serving, 6 servings per recipe: Calories: 219. Protein: 11g. Total fat: 9.3g (sat. fat: 5.2g). Carbohydrates: 22g. Cholesterol: 106mg. Sodium: 300mg. Vitamin A: 17% DV. Vitamin C: 26% DV.

The success of this soup depends on the richness of the broth, the sweetness of the onion, and the beauty of the presentation.

French Onion Soup

2 tablespoons butter or olive oil
3 large onions, chopped coarsely
6 cups vegetable broth*
¼ cup dry white wine
1 bay leaf
¾ teaspoon salt
freshly ground black pepper to taste
6 slices of French bread, toasted
6 ounces Gruyere or other Swiss cheese, grated

Melt butter in a soup pot over medium-low heat. Add onions and sauté, stirring often, until golden brown and tender, approximately 15 to 20 minutes. If onions begin to stick, add a few tablespoons of the broth. When onions are ready, add broth, wine, bay leaf, salt, and pepper. Allow soup to slowly simmer for 30 minutes. To serve, ladle soup into individual ovenproof bowls, place a slice of French bread on top of the soup, and sprinkle with 1 ounce of the cheese. Place soup under broiler just long enough for cheese to melt and become bubbly. Serve immediately. Serves 6.

*The flavor of this simple soup depends greatly on the quality and flavor of the broth you use. For a brief description of how to make vegetable broth refer to page 206 .

Nutrition information per serving, 6 servings per recipe: Calories: 317. Protein: 16g. Total fat: 15.6g (sat. fat: 6.2g). Carbohydrates: 32g. Cholesterol: 31mg. Sodium: 748mg. Vitamin A: 40% DV. Vitamin C: 13% DV.

NUTRITION INFORMATION PER ½ CUP ONION, COOKED:

Calories: 29
Total fat: <0.2g
(saturated fat: 0g)
Fiber: 1.4g
Sodium: 8mg
Potassium: 5% Daily Value
Vitamin A: 0% Daily Value
Vitamin C: 10% Daily Value
Iron: 1% Daily Value
Calcium: 3% Daily Value

PEPPERS

FRYING PEPPERS
are what we call those sweet peppers that are generally smaller than bell peppers, more conical in shape, with a much thinner wall. They are usually light green or red and have a more delicate taste than bell peppers. Admittedly, these peppers take a little more work to prepare simply because they are smaller, but you will be rewarded by their subtle taste. Fryers are best showcased in Italian sandwiches, where the flavor is enhanced by a light sautéeing. They also are wonderful in salads or simmered in a delicious red sauce.

HANDLING: In general, peppers keep well for several days in the refrigerator. Frying peppers, having thinner walls, tend to wilt or pucker more quickly. Use them soon after harvest. If you find yourself with a surplus, consider freezing them. Follow the directions for freezing bell peppers. Like bells, frying peppers will be soft when thawed but are perfect for use in a slow-simmered red pasta sauce.

SIMPLE PREPARATION: Like most sweet peppers, fryers are delicious raw, especially when they are fresh from the garden. After a careful washing, remove the stem end, slice lengthwise, and then remove the seeds and ribs. Cut into long slivers and use to garnish a green salad or as part of a vegetable platter. Sautéeing or "frying" these delicate peppers is probably the best way to enjoy their subtle flavor. Heat a small amount of olive oil in a skillet over medium heat and slowly sauté pepper slivers until tender and sweet—so much the better if you have a variety of colors of peppers. Sautéed peppers are delicious in an omelet or a frittata, combined with cooked corn kernels, cannellini beans, and a few fresh herbs and seasonings for an easy salad, or as an embellishment on grilled veggie burgers.

Frittatas are a great company dish—beautifully golden when made with farm-fresh eggs, accepting of almost any vegetable you'd like to include. Particularly impressive when baked in a cast iron skillet. This recipe is most attractive if you use a combination of red and green peppers.

Frittata with Sweet Peppers and Summer Squash

1 tablespoon olive oil
4 green onions, chopped
4 frying peppers, seeded and chopped
2 small zucchini, chopped (nice to have one each of green and golden)
2 teaspoons finely minced fresh oregano
¾ teaspoon salt
6 eggs
½ cup lowfat milk
½ cup grated Fontina cheese
¼ cup freshly grated Parmesan cheese
freshly ground black pepper

Heat olive oil in a medium-sized skillet over medium heat. Add onions and lightly sauté for 1 minute. Add peppers, zucchini, oregano, and ¼ teaspoon of the salt. Sauté for 4 to 5 minutes longer or until zucchini is just beginning to brown. Remove from heat and set aside. Preheat oven to 350°F. Beat eggs with milk and the remaining ½ teaspoon of salt. Add the cheeses and black pepper. Stir in the vegetable mixture. Pour into a lightly oiled 10-inch round baking dish or cast iron skillet and bake for approximately 40 minutes or until just set. Cut into wedges and serve hot from the oven. Serves 6.

Nutrition information per serving, 6 servings per recipe: Calories: 179. Protein: 13g. Total fat: 11.5g (sat. fat: 4.9g). Carbohydrates: 5g. Cholesterol: 182mg. Sodium: 489mg. Vitamin A: 30% DV. Vitamin C: 119% DV.

In the heat of the summer, when it's too hot to cook, put together these attractive and delicious sandwiches. You'll need to find really good Italian rolls—chewy, crusty, and very fresh. Serve with a small green salad and a tall glass of lemonade.

Fresh Mozzarella and Pepper Sandwiches

1 teaspoon olive oil
4 frying peppers, sliced in slivers
several leaves of fresh oregano, minced
4 soft Italian rolls
6 ounces fresh Mozzarella, sliced
8 to 12 slices garden-fresh tomatoes
fresh basil leaves
2 to 3 tablespoons pesto

Heat olive oil in a small skillet over medium heat. Add peppers and fresh oregano. Sauté until just tender-crisp. Remove from heat and set aside. Slice rolls in half. Arrange slices of Mozzarella, tomatoes, and basil leaves artistically on bottom half of bun. Mound sautéed peppers on top. Top with several teaspoons of pesto. Serve with top half of roll on the side. Beautiful! Makes 4 sandwiches.

Nutrition information per sandwich: Calories: 337. Protein: 18g. Total fat: 12g (sat. fat: 5.4g). Carbohydrates: 37g. Cholesterol: 25.2mg. Sodium: 568mg. Vitamin A: 19% DV. Vitamin C: 177% DV.

NUTRITION INFORMATION PER 1 LARGE FRYING PEPPER, RAW:

Calories: 18
Total fat: <0.2g
    (saturated fat: 0g)
Fiber: 1.1g
Sodium: 2mg
Potassium: 4% Daily Value
Vitamin A: 4% Daily Value
Vitamin C: 158% Daily Value
Iron: 5% Daily Value
Calcium: <1% Daily Value

PEPPERS

HOT PEPPERS

HOT PEPPERS, or chilis, are small but mighty members of the *Capsicum* genus.
What makes your mouth burn when you eat hot peppers are capsaicinoids, which are mostly
concentrated in the skin, seeds, and interior ribs of hot peppers. Capsaicinoids are odorless and
tasteless. They react directly with the pain receptors in your mouth. Perhaps you've experienced
this firsthand with, say, a fresh habañero—the hottest of the hot. Of course, not all hot peppers
are created equal. Some, like Anaheim peppers, are relatively mild and are the choice for the
classic Mexican dish Chiles Rellenos. Deep green, pudgy jalapeños have a powerful bite and
are one of the more familiar hot peppers. Serranos are sleek and delicate-looking, but don't be
misled by their appearance—these peppers are extremely fiery. With over 50 varieties of hot
peppers available, the possibilities of spicing up your life are great. Just proceed with caution!

HANDLING: Like all peppers, hot peppers should be firm and glossy. If you intend to use
them fresh, they should be stored in the refrigerator. Fully mature peppers can also be dried.
String them together by sewing through the stems, allowing room between the peppers for air to
circulate. Hang strung peppers in a cool, dry, airy spot. The real challenge of handling hot
peppers comes when you want to prepare them for a recipe. It's best to wear rubber or plastic
gloves when working with hot peppers. Don't use your kitchen cutting board to work on—the
residues will contaminate everything you prepare afterward. Work on a glass plate that can be
washed easily, or on a clean piece of cardboard that you can throw away. When cutting into a hot
pepper, be cautious of the seeds, which can easily pop out.

SIMPLE PREPARATION: Some like it hot—and if you're one of them, you might enjoy slices
of fresh hot pepper served up with your nachos or tacos. Probably the most common use of hot
peppers is in fresh salsa. If you've never made fresh salsa you're in for a treat the first time you
do. The taste is so light and fresh, and the process is so simple, that you'll want to do it as long
as garden tomatoes and peppers are in season. With a snip of hot pepper, a splash of lime juice,
and a sprinkle of cilantro, you can easily change the nationality of your favorite pasta dish.

Hot, freshly made corn tortillas. A pot of perfectly seasoned black beans. Slices of ripe avocados. A big bowl of fresh salsa. A feast!

Salsa Nancita

5 medium tomatoes, peeled, seeded, finely chopped
1 sweet green pepper, minced
1 small onion, minced
2 tablespoons chopped fresh parsley
2 tablespoons chopped fresh cilantro
1 hot pepper, cored, seeded, minced
½ teaspoon ground cumin
¾ teaspoon salt
1 tablespoon honey or other sweetener
1 to 2 tablespoons fresh lime juice

Mix ingredients together well, allow to sit for 1 to 2 hours before serving. Makes 6 servings.

Nutrition information per serving, 6 servings per recipe: Calories: 42. Protein: 1g. Total fat: <1g (sat. fat: 0g). Carbohydrates: 10g. Cholesterol: 0mg. Sodium: 270mg. Vitamin A: 17% DV. Vitamin C: 65% DV.

There's a time in the summer when the vegetables and herbs in this dish show up at the farmers' market together. Gather them up and bring them home to prepare a tasty and spicy pasta meal.

Pasta with Spicy Summer Vegetables

1 pound penne pasta*
3 ears of corn (or 1¼ cups corn kernels, frozen or canned)
2 tablespoons olive oil
3 to 4 cloves garlic, minced or pressed
1 green or red sweet pepper, chopped
1 or 2 hot peppers, seeded & chopped
⅓ cup sun-dried tomatoes, soaked in boiling water, drained, and chopped
1 medium zucchini, chopped
2 medium tomatoes, diced
⅓ cup white wine (water or vegetable stock may be substituted)
2 tablespoons chopped cilantro (more or less according to your taste)
2 to 3 tablespoons chopped fresh basil
2 green onions, thinly sliced
1 tablespoon fresh lime juice
1 teaspoon salt
freshly ground black pepper to taste

Put on a large pot of water and cook the pasta while you prepare the vegetable topping. If using fresh corn, cut corn from the ears and discard cobs. Set aside. In a large skillet, warm the olive oil over medium heat. Add the garlic and sauté for 1 minute. Add the sweet and hot peppers and sauté for 2 minutes. Add sun-dried tomatoes and zucchini. Sauté 2 to 3 more minutes. Add corn kernels, diced fresh tomatoes, wine or stock, and simmer 2 to 3 minutes. Stir in cilantro, basil, green onions, lime juice, salt, and black pepper. Simmer for 1 minute. Serve over hot pasta. Pass the Parmesan. Serve with chewy Italian or crusty French bread. Serves 6 to 8.

*Penne is a thin tube-shaped pasta with diagonally cut ends. It is my preference for this recipe although other shapes such as bowties or rigatoni will also do. Whatever shape you use be sure to choose a high quality pasta.

Nutritional information per serving, 6 servings per recipe: Calories: 224. Protein: 6g. Total fat: 4.7g (sat. fat: <1g). Carbohydrates: 37g. Cholesterol: 0mg. Sodium: 368mg. Vitamin A: 15% DV. Vitamin C: 128% DV.

Here's an intriguing combination of apples, onions, and jalapeño pepper in a salad that's delicious served as a side dish with Indian or Mexican food.

Apple Salad with Jalapeño-Lime Dressing

3 cups cubed firm, sweet apple
1 cup coarsely chopped red onion
1 jalapeño pepper, cored, seeded, minced
1 teaspoon canola oil
3 tablespoons lime juice
1 teaspoon honey or brown sugar
¼ teaspoon salt
⅛ teaspoon freshly ground cumin seed

Combine apples, onions, and jalapeño pepper together in a medium-sized bowl. Combine remaining ingredients and pour over apple mixture. Toss to coat apples. Chill well. Serves 4.

Nutritional information per serving, 4 servings per recipe: Calories: 85. Protein: 1g. Total fat: 1.3g (sat. fat: <1g). Carbohydrates: 17g. Cholesterol: 0mg. Sodium: 135mg. Vitamin A: 1% DV. Vitamin C: 70% DV.

NUTRITION INFORMATION PER ½ CUP HOT PEPPER, RAW:

Calories: 30
Total fat: <0.2g
   (saturated fat: 0g)
Fiber: 0.7g
Sodium: 5mg
Potassium: 7% Daily Value
Vitamin A: 81% Daily Value
Vitamin C: 303% Daily Value
Iron: 5% Daily Value
Calcium: 1% Daily Value

HOT PEPPERS

PEPPERS

SWEET BELL PEPPERS are the large box-shape peppers most popular in
the United States, accounting for more than 60 percent of the domestic pepper crop. Although
we commonly refer to this *Capsicum annuum* as green pepper, bell peppers also come in
yellow, orange, red, and less common white, deep purple, and chocolate. Bell peppers have no
relation to *Piper nigrum,* or what we commonly call black pepper. It appears this misnomer is
the result of Christopher Columbus's search for the black pepper of India. What he found was
the New World, with a wonderful cuisine that included the taste of *Capsicum annuum,* a plant
native to the Americas. He carried the seeds of what he called the "pepper" plant back to Spain,
where they were integrated into Old World cuisine. The name stuck—at least in our culture.

HANDLING: Bell peppers are fairly patient and will last for up to a week in the refrigerator,
especially if they are garden-fresh. Since red bell peppers are more mature than green peppers,
they won't last quite as long. There is a significant difference in taste and texture between
fresh-from-the-garden peppers and shipped-halfway-across-the-country peppers. Fresh peppers
are sweet, juicy, and crisp. If you hold a slice of bell pepper up to the light and bend it slightly,
you will see a mist of water spraying from it—snapping with freshness when you bend it too
far. Older peppers, which still add flavor to dishes when you sauté them, lack the vitality and
delectable nature of really fresh bells.

SIMPLE PREPARATION: Peppers are wonderful raw—chopped in a variety of cold salads, as
whole rings on sandwiches, or as long slivers on a vegetable plate with or without dip. Sautéeing
changes their character and opens up a whole new world of culinary options. Peppers and onions
are an unbeatable combination in scrambled eggs and omelets, in spaghetti sauce, and as the
starring vegetables in fajitas. Roasting elevates peppers to the role of a gourmet food. If you
have an abundance of peppers, consider freezing them. Wash your peppers, seed, mince or chop,
and freeze in sealed bags or small containers—no need to blanch first. Freezing breaks down
the texture of peppers but the taste is still there for use in recipes where peppers will be cooked.

In this homey recipe, green peppers are filled with a light mixture of orzo, vegetables, and sharp Cheddar.

Peppers Stuffed with Orzo and Sharp Cheddar Cheese

4 large bell peppers
½ cup orzo, cooked, and drained
1 tablespoon olive oil
3 cloves garlic, minced or pressed
1 small onion, chopped
2 carrots, chopped
1 medium zucchini, chopped
2 tablespoons white wine or water
4 tablespoons chopped fresh parsley
4 tablespoons chopped fresh basil
½ teaspoon salt
freshly ground black pepper
4 ounces sharp Cheddar cheese, shredded

Cut the tops from the peppers, remove the interior ribs and seeds. Save the tops—these will be chopped up and added to the filling. Very lightly steam or blanch the peppers—they should still be bright green and firm. Remove from steamer basket or water, turn upside down and allow to drain while you prepare the filling. Heat the oil over medium heat in a large skillet. Add the garlic and onions and sauté for 5 minutes. Add the carrots, zucchini, and the chopped pepper tops. Sauté for 2 to 3 minutes longer. Add the white wine or water. Cover, and steam over medium heat for approximately 5 to 7 minutes, or until vegetables are tender-crisp. Remove from heat. Toss in the cooked orzo, parsley, and basil. Season with salt and pepper. Carefully toss in the cheese. Preheat oven to 350°F. Place whole peppers upright in a small baking dish. Divide the filling in four and stuff the peppers. Pour ¼ cup water in the bottom of the pan with the peppers and cover. Bake until peppers are just tender-crisp, and stuffing is thoroughly warmed, approximately 20 to 30 minutes. Remove peppers carefully from baking dish and allow to sit on a plate for 5 minutes before serving—this will allow excess water to drain. Serves 4.

Nutrition information per serving, 4 servings per recipe: Calories: 196. Protein: 10g. Total fat: 8.9g (sat. fat: 3.5g). Carbohydrates: 17g. Cholesterol: 20mg. Sodium: 531mg. Vitamin A: 114% DV. Vitamin C: 182% DV.

In 1993, Community Mercantile Co-op in Lawrence, Kansas moved into a beautiful new storefront. There was cause to celebrate—not only our expansion and relocation, but also nineteen years of serving our community. There were weeks and weeks of grand opening galas and in-store samplings. The Veggie Fajitas still stand out in my mind as the favorite of all the samplings.

Veggie Fajitas

Marinade:

3 tablespoons reduced-sodium soy sauce
2 tablespoons cider vinegar
juice of 1 lime
1 tablespoon fajita seasoning mix

½ pound seitan* (wheat gluten) cut into strips
1 tablespoon canola oil
2 large green bell peppers, cut into strips
1 large red bell pepper, cut into strips
2 medium-sized onions, cut into slivers
big flour tortillas
salsa
plain yogurt or lowfat sour cream

Mix together the marinade ingredients. Add seitan strips and allow to marinate for 15 minutes. Heat oil in a large skillet or wok over medium-high heat. Add pepper strips and onions. Cook, stirring constantly, for 2 to 3 minutes. Add seitan with marinade. Cook for 3 to 4 minutes more until steaming hot but vegetables are still crunchy. Serve on big flour tortillas with salsa. Nice with a dollop of yogurt or lowfat sour cream. Serves 4.

*Seitan is made from the glutenous part of wheat. It is very high in protein and extremely low in fat, with no cholesterol. Seitan is available in the refrigerated section of natural food stores and some Oriental markets.

Nutrition information per serving, 4 servings per recipe: Calories: 153. Protein: 18g. Total fat: 3.4g (sat. fat: <1g). Carbohydrates: 11g. Cholesterol: 0mg. Sodium: 573mg. Vitamin A: 15% DV. Vitamin C: 155% DV.

Roasted Red Peppers

Roasted red peppers are really quite the rage, showing up in all kinds of recipes—on sandwiches, in hummus, in salads. And no wonder. Sweet, crunchy red peppers are delicious, but the roasting process deepens and mellows their flavor and texture. If you have a gas range you can hold the pepper (with tongs is easiest) over the flame, turning until the skin is darkened evenly all over. Place the charred pepper in a covered bowl or plastic bag and allow to steam in its own heat for 10 to 15 minutes. Remove from bowl or bag and scrape off the darkened skin with a dull knife. Cut open the pepper and remove the veins and seeds. You can also grill peppers outside on a charcoal fire in the same manner. Lacking a gas range or charcoal fire, peppers can easily be roasted in the oven. The flavor won't be quite the same but the end effect is similar and your kitchen will smell wonderful while the peppers are roasting. Preheat oven to 450°F. Cut peppers in half lengthwise, clean out veins and seeds. Rub the outside of the pepper with a little olive oil. Place cut side down in a baking dish and bake until pepper begins to wilt and slightly darkens, approximately 20 minutes. Remove from oven and place in covered bowl. Remove skins as described above.

NUTRITION INFORMATION PER ½ CUP BELL PEPPERS, RAW:

Calories: 12
Total fat: <0.2g
    (saturated fat: 0g)
Fiber: 0.8g
Sodium: 2mg
Potassium: 3% Daily Value
Vitamin A: 3% Daily Value
Vitamin C: 107% Daily Value
Iron: 3% Daily Value
Calcium: <1% Daily Value

PEPPERS

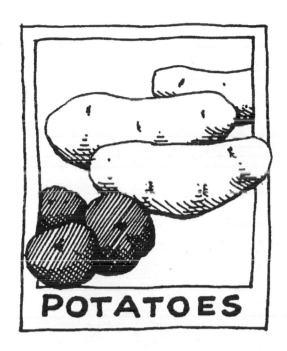

POTATOES

POTATOES hardly need an introduction. They are the most widely consumed
vegetable in the world and the most popular vegetable in the United States, with an average
annual per capita consumption of 126 pounds. This member of the nightshade family is a native
of South America. It was introduced to Europe in 1570 and found its way to North America in
the early 1700s. Potatoes played such an important part in the survival of Irish peasants in the
mid-1800s that when the potato blight struck in 1845 and 1846, millions of peasants died of
starvation or were forced to emigrate from Ireland. There are many varieties of potatoes. When
choosing potatoes for a recipe, consider whether you want a starchy potato such as a russet for
baking, or a waxy potato like a red potato that will hold its shape in such dishes as potato salad.
New potatoes aren't a specific variety. Rather, they are freshly dug, never-been-stored potatoes.
Their skins are thin and easily rub off. New potatoes have a higher moisture and sugar content,
so they cook more quickly and have a sweeter taste than storage potatoes.

HANDLING: Potatoes should be firm and free of sprouts. It is also important that they do not
have a greenish tinge. This indicates the presence of solanine, a naturally occurring toxin. Store
potatoes in a dark, dry place, since light and warmth encourage the development of solanine.
Potatoes don't care for the cold so don't put them in the refrigerator—this causes the starches to
convert to sugar. Although many cooks store potatoes and onions together, it is best to keep them
separate. Onions give off gases that accelerate the decay of potatoes. Wash your potatoes well,
but not until you're ready to use them. Carefully cut out any bad spots, bruises, or green spots.

SIMPLE PREPARATION: Many elaborate dishes can be made with potatoes, but nothing is
easier than a baked potato. Pierce potato with a fork to allow steam to escape. Bake until tender
in a 400°F oven, 45 to 60 minutes, depending on size. Top with yogurt or low-fat sour cream
and snips of fresh chives. Mashed potatoes are another all-American favorite. No need to peel
potatoes, especially when they are organically grown—the skins add texture, color, and fiber.
Add roasted garlic (see page 110) for a rich and special flavor.

Of the many, many Rolling Prairie recipes that have been sampled over the past five years, this soup stands out as one of the all time favorites.

Potato, Corn, and Cheese Chowder

    3 medium potatoes, scrubbed and diced
    3 cups water
    1 bay leaf
    ½ teaspoon salt
    1 tablespoon canola oil
    1 medium onion, finely chopped
    3 tablespoons unbleached white flour
    1½ cups lowfat milk
    1½ cups corn kernels (fresh or frozen)
    ½ teaspoon ground cumin
    1 tablespoon fresh chives, chopped (or 1 teaspoon dried chives)
    ¼ cup chopped parsley
    scant ¼ teaspoon ground nutmeg
    ¼ teaspoon black pepper
    4 ounces reduced-fat Cheddar cheese, grated

Boil diced potatoes in water with bay leaf and ¼ teaspoon salt until barely tender. While potatoes are cooking, sauté onions in oil over medium-low heat until tender and nearly transparent (add a few tablespoons of water if onions begin to stick). Add flour to sautéed onions and mix thoroughly. Add milk gradually, stirring constantly. Pour this mixture slowly into the cooked potatoes and their water, along with the corn kernels. Add cumin, chives, parsley, nutmeg, the remaining ¼ teaspoon salt, and pepper. Let the soup simmer over very low heat for approximately 15 minutes. Add in the grated cheese and stir until completely melted. If chowder seems too thick, thin with milk or water. Serve immediately. Serves 4.

Nutrition information per serving, 4 servings per recipe: Calories: 310. Protein: 17g. Total fat: 8.9g (sat. fat: 3.3g). Carbohydrates: 38g. Cholesterol: 22.5mg. Sodium: 571mg. Vitamin A: 24% DV. Vitamin C: 24% DV.

This potato salad is reminiscent of what I ate at picnics and family get-togethers when I was growing up. It is fashioned after my Aunt Marge's famous potato salad which contained her "secret ingredient"—pickle juice. Definitely not necessary but it does help thin the salad dressing. You could substitute a very mild vinegar.

The Simplest Spud Salad

2 to 2½ pounds waxy potatoes (either new potatoes, red potatoes, or fingerlings)
2 tablespoons minced onion
3 medium carrots, coarsely grated
6 stalks celery, chopped
½ cup salad dressing*
2 tablespoons mustard
2 tablespoons pickle juice
1½ teaspoons salt
freshly ground black pepper to taste

Cook potatoes until just tender but not falling apart. Cut into large chunks. Allow to cool. Toss potatoes with onions, carrots and celery. Mix salad dressing, mustard, and pickle juice together. Pour over potato mixture, sprinkle on salt and pepper and carefully toss until veggies are well coated with dressing. Refrigerate for several hours. Serves 8.

*For my salad dressing I use Nayonaise®, a dressing made from tofu. It is relatively low in fat, contains no cholesterol, and has a nice light taste. You could also use a light mayonnaise.

Nutrition information per serving, 8 servings per recipe: Calories: 182. Protein: 2g. Total fat: 3.7g (sat. fat: 0g). Carbohydrates: 33g. Cholesterol: 0mg. Sodium: 585mg. Vitamin A: 76% DV. Vitamin C: 40% DV.

NUTRITION INFORMATION PER 1 LARGE POTATO, BAKED:

Calories: 220
Total fat: <0.2g
(saturated fat: 0g)
Fiber: 5g
Sodium: 16mg
Potassium: 24% Daily Value
Vitamin A: 0% Daily Value
Vitamin C: 43% Daily Value
Iron: 16% Daily Value
Calcium: 2% Daily Value

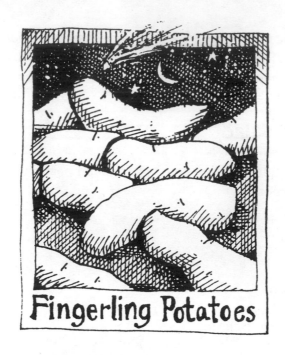

Fingerling Potatoes

FINGERLING POTATOES

FINGERLING POTATOES are small, elongated tubers—slender, like fingers. Honestly, I had never heard of fingerlings, never mind eaten them, until I was introduced to them through the Rolling Prairie Farmers Alliance. I immediately fell in love with them. Their size makes them perfect for roasting and boiling whole. The taste and texture are everything I want in a potato—flavorful, moist, thin skinned, easy to prepare. And they're cute. Fingerlings are much more common in Europe, with names like Swedish Peanut, Russian Banana, and Rose Fin Apple. Unless you have the good fortune to be a member of a CSA program like Rolling Prairie, or regularly shop at a farmers' market, you may never get to experience these little treasures. They are worth seeking out.

HANDLING: Just like full-sized potatoes, fingerlings should be solid and firm, not tinged with green. Treat fingerling potatoes like new potatoes—use them soon after they come into your possession. Right before you're ready to use them, wash the fingerlings carefully—their skin can be tender and will peel off with too vigorous a scrubbing.

SIMPLE PREPARATION: The beauty of fingerlings is how easy they are to prepare. Boil them whole, cut in half or thirds, toss with a little olive oil, salt and pepper. Enjoy. Because of their more waxy character, fingerlings are a good choice for home fries. Sauté chopped onions in a little olive oil. Add slices of fingerling potatoes. Stir over medium heat and cook until potatoes are just tender. Season with salt and pepper and a snip of fresh dill or minced fresh rosemary.

Mark Lumpe, with help from wife Julie and daughter Emma, runs Wakarusa Valley certified organic farm, outside Lawrence, Kansas. Mark is one of the original growers in the Rolling Prairie Farmers Alliance. This recipe was the result of a stop at the Wakarusa Valley produce stand at the Lawrence Farmers' Market and is a tribute to the beautiful vegetables Mark and Julie grow.

Lumpy (Lumpe) Burritos

1 to 1½ pounds new potatoes or fingerling potatoes
1 tablespoon oil
1 medium-sized onion, chopped
1 green or red bell pepper, chopped
½ teaspoon ground cumin
½ teaspoon salt
pepper to taste
2 to 4 tablespoons each chopped fresh parsley and cilantro
8 to 10 large flour tortillas
1½ cups refried beans
1½ cups grated lowfat cheese (Mozzarella, Cheddar, Jack, or Jalapeño Jack)
tomatoes, yogurt or sour cream, and salsa for garnish

Wash the potatoes, cut into large cubes, cover with water in a large pot, and boil until just tender but still firm. If you're using fingerling potatoes, the tiny ones can be boiled whole and the larger ones cut up in several pieces. While the potatoes are boiling, heat the oil in a large skillet over medium heat and sauté the onion and pepper until just tender. Preheat oven to 350°F. When the potatoes are done, drain well and add to the onion-pepper mixture. Sprinkle with cumin, salt, and pepper. Continue to cook, stirring frequently until the potatoes begin to brown. Remove from heat. Toss in chopped parsley and cilantro. To assemble your burritos, lay out a tortilla, place approximately 2 to 3 tablespoons refried beans down the center, top with a generous helping of the potatoes, sprinkle on 2 to 3 tablespoons of cheese, and roll up as tightly as you can—they will be rather lumpy looking. Place in an ungreased 9 x 13-inch baking dish. Continue making burritos until you've used up all your filling, lining them up in your baking dish as you make them. Bake for 20 minutes. Serve hot, topped with chopped fresh tomatoes, a dollop of plain yogurt or light sour cream, and salsa. Makes 8 to10 burritos.

Nutrition information per serving, 8 servings per recipe: Calories: 260. Protein: 10g. Total fat: 6.5g (sat. fat: 2.3g). Carbohydrates: 39g. Cholesterol: 13mg. Sodium: 531mg. Vitamin A: 4% DV. Vitamin C: 45% DV.

Little jewels of potatoes tossed with olive oil and fresh basil, punctuated by bits of sun-dried tomatoes—potato salad at its best!

Fingerling Potato Salad

⅓ cup finely chopped sun-dried tomatoes
1 to 1½ pounds fingerling potatoes
1 cup finely chopped green onions
¼ cup minced fresh basil
½ teaspoon ground cumin
3 tablespoons olive oil
2 tablespoons fresh lemon juice or 2 tablespoons balsamic vinegar
½ teaspoon salt
lots of freshly ground black pepper

Cover the sun-dried tomatoes with boiling water and set aside. Wash the fingerling potatoes and boil in their skins until just tender but not falling apart. Drain thoroughly. Cut larger potatoes in 2 or 3 pieces. Leave the smallest ones whole. Drain tomatoes and press out excess water. Combine tomatoes with potatoes and toss with remaining ingredients. Serve at room temperature. Serves 5.

Nutrition information per serving, 5 servings per recipe: Calories: 201. Protein: 2g. Total fat: 7.6 g (sat. fat: 1.1g). Carbohydrates: 30g. Cholesterol: 0mg. Sodium: 222mg. Vitamin A: 14% DV. Vitamin C: 57% DV.

Here are some very general directions for the pairing of potatoes and green beans in a simple yet satisfying dish. You can determine exact amounts. Just a note about the tarragon—it is a very distinctive herb with a taste that can overpower. It's best to start with a small amount.

Herbed Fingerling Potatoes with Green Beans

Wash fingerling potatoes and cut in 1-inch sections, leaving tiny potatoes whole. Wash and trim ends of green beans but leave full length. Mince ½ of a small onion. Heat 1 to 2 tablespoons olive oil in a large skillet over medium heat. Add onions and sauté for 1 to 2 minutes. Add potatoes and sauté for 3 to 4 more minutes. Add several tablespoons water to skillet, reduce heat to medium-low, cover, and cook until potatoes are just about tender. Add more water if necessary. Add green beans, several tablespoons of chopped fresh basil, a smaller amount of snipped fresh tarragon (or dried if fresh isn't available), season with salt and pepper and cook, covered, just long enough to steam the beans tender-crisp. Feel free to add a splash of balsamic vinegar right before serving.

NUTRITION INFORMATION PER 4 FINGERLINGS, BOILED:

Calories: 220
Total fat: <0.2g
     (saturated fat: 0g)
Fiber: 5g
Sodium: 16mg
Potassium: 24% Daily Value
Vitamin A: 0% Daily Value
Vitamin C: 43% Daily Value
Iron: 16% Daily Value
Calcium: 2% Daily Value

Fingerling Potatoes

PIE PUMPKINS

PUMPKINS are one of my favorites vegetables. Unlike the demanding and
perishable vegetables of summer, pumpkins will wait patiently, sometimes for months, to be
transformed into pie or stew. And while they're waiting, they look absolutely homey and lovely
sitting around the kitchen. Pumpkins are native to the Americas and were partly responsible for
the survival of the first Pilgrims. American Indians had long cultivated this member of the
Cucurbit family, and the cousin of melon, winter squash, and gourd. They knew how to grow it
between the rows of beans and corn. There are many varieties of pumpkins. Some are bred for
their size, destined to become jack-o'-lanterns on Halloween—their flesh is stringy and not very
tasty. Pie pumpkins are usually small, with a tender and sweet flesh. There is nothing quite like
the taste of homemade pumpkin pie made with fresh pumpkin—not to mention the delicious
and festive smell while the pie is baking!

HANDLING: No special procedures here—pumpkins will keep for several months in a dry,
ventilated area.

SIMPLE PREPARATION: Don't hesitate to cook your beautiful pumpkin to make a pie—it is a
simple process that just takes a little time. Slice the pumpkin in half lengthwise with a stout
knife. Scoop out the stringy pulp and seeds with a metal spoon. Cut each half into 6 or 8 pieces
and steam until tender. If you have a pressure cooker, this will only take about 15 minutes under
pressure. Otherwise, steam until flesh is soft, about 45 minutes (take care not to run out of
water). Pumpkin can also be baked like other hard squashes in a 350°F oven for about an hour.
After cooking, separate pieces and allow to cool—we lay the pieces directly on the kitchen
counter. Then scrape the cooked pumpkin off the tough outer skin and use in your recipe.

There is nothing quite as comforting as sweet, creamy pumpkin pie or raisin-studded pumpkin bread. But pumpkin really is a versatile vegetable—equally at home in both sweet and savory dishes. It can be used in almost any recipe calling for butternut squash. Pumpkins generally have a deeper, more earthy taste than butternut—just fine for a hearty stew on a chilly evening.

Black Bean and Pumpkin Stew

2 tablespoons olive oil
3 cups pumpkin, peeled and cut into 1/2-inch cubes
4 cloves garlic, minced
1 large onion, diced
1 to 2 hot peppers (to taste), seeded and finely minced
¾ teaspoon ground cumin
½ teaspoon ground cinnamon
¼ teaspoon ground cloves
1 teaspoon chili powder
1 teaspoon salt
1 28-ounce can plum tomatoes, chopped
½ cup dry red wine or vegetable broth
3½ cups vegetable broth
4 cups cooked black beans, rinsed and drained
2 cups corn kernels, fresh off the cob or frozen
sour cream and fresh cilantro for garnish

Heat 1 tablespoon of the olive oil in a large heavy skillet over medium heat. Add the pumpkin and sauté until beginning to brown, approximately 10 minutes. Set aside. In a large soup pot, heat remaining oil over medium heat. Add garlic, onion, and hot pepper. Sauté until just beginning to get tender. Add cumin, cinnamon, cloves, chili powder, and salt. Stir to combine. Add tomatoes and their juice, along with the wine and/or broth, and the sautéed pumpkin. Bring to a boil, reduce heat and allow to simmer 20 minutes. Add beans and corn. Simmer for another 20 minutes, adding more broth if necessary to thin the stew. Serve hot, with a spoonful of sour cream and chopped fresh cilantro for garnish. Serves 6 to 8.

Nutrition information per serving, 6 servings per recipe: Calories: 362. Protein: 15g. Total fat: 5.7g (sat. fat: 1.1g). Carbohydrates: 62g. Cholesterol: <1mg. Sodium: 605mg. Vitamin A: 52% DV. Vitamin C: 84% DV.

In this particular recipe, the pumpkin pie filling is completely fat free, all of the fat is found in the crust. There are those times when you really want to splurge with a crust, but consider baking this pumpkin pie filling directly in a baking dish. You'll have a really nutritious dessert that you can serve up as a pudding ... and you may not even miss the crust!

Pumpkin Pie

2 cups cooked pumpkin, winter squash, or sweet potatoes
½ cup honey or maple syrup
3 egg whites
1½ cups evaporated skimmed milk or regular lowfat milk
1 teaspoon cinnamon
½ teaspoon ground ginger
¼ teaspoon ground cloves
½ teaspoon salt
1 9-inch unbaked whole wheat pie crust

Preheat oven to 425°F. Place all filling ingredients in blender and blend until smooth. Pour into 9-inch unbaked pie crust and bake for 15 minutes at 425°F. Reduce temperature to 350°F and bake another 45 minutes or until set. Makes one 9-inch pie.

Nutrition information per serving, 8 servings per pie, baked in a crust: Calories: 232. Protein: 7g. Total fat: 6.2g (sat. fat: <1g). Carbohydrates: 36g. Cholesterol: 1.5mg. Sodium: 410mg. Vitamin A: 12% DV. Vitamin C: 5% DV.

NUTRITION INFORMATION PER ½ CUP PIE PUMPKIN, COOKED:

Calories: 24
Total fat: 0g
  (saturated fat: 0g)
Fiber: 3.5g
Sodium: 2mg
Potassium: 8% Daily Value
Vitamin A: 13% Daily Value
Vitamin C: 10% Daily Value
Iron: 4% Daily Value
Calcium: 2% Daily Value

PIE PUMPKINS

RADISHES

RADISHES are a sign of spring. When they are grown with care, and harvested young, they are a versatile and delicious vegetable—not just an adornment for the vegetable platter. This little cruciferous vegetable, related to broccoli and kale, has a long history of cultivation. Native to China, radishes were also enjoyed in Egypt and Greece. Purportedly, builders of the Great Pyramid dined on radishes, onions, and garlic—quite a diet! In addition to the familiar red globe, radishes come in white and black, long and narrow. In Europe, radishes are served whole on buttered French bread. In China and Japan, they are eaten in large quantities fresh, cooked, and pickled. We have some catching up to do.

HANDLING: Radishes should be solid and firm. Red radishes shouldn't be much bigger than 1½ -inches in diameter or most likely they will be pithy. If your radishes come with the green tops, remove them before storing—they will keep better if separated from the greens. Radish greens, if crisp and fresh, can be prepared like any other leafy green. Stored in a plastic bag, radishes will keep in the refrigerator for up to two weeks—a durable little vegetable.

SIMPLE PREPARATION: Wash and eat, greens and all, if they're fresh from the garden. Radish slices add color and crunch to green salad and potato salad. Grated radish can be added to coleslaw or carrot salad, or mixed with lowfat sour cream to use as a dip or garnish. If you have an abundance of radishes, experiment with cooking them. Although most of us probably think of radishes as a vegetable eaten raw, they can also be steamed or sautéed—prepared this way they have a texture and taste similar to white turnips.

Radishes and green onions are both early garden offerings. Here they are paired in a snappy mixture that can be tucked in the pocket of a pita or added to a simple green salad to serve as the embellishment and the dressing. If you think you don't care much for radishes, give this recipe a try. It may change your thinking!

Radishes and Green Onions with Feta cheese

    2 cups thinly-sliced radishes
    3 or 4 green onions, finely chopped
    4 ounces Feta cheese, crumbled
    10 to 12 Kalamata olives, pitted, and chopped coarsely
    1 tablespoon chopped fresh mint
    ¼ teaspoon salt
    freshly ground black pepper
    1½ tablespoons olive oil
    1 tablespoon freshly-squeezed lemon juice

Toss together the radishes, green onions, Feta cheese, olives, and fresh mint. Season with the salt and pepper. Toss again. Whisk the olive oil and lemon juice together and pour over the vegetable mixture. Toss to coat vegetables with dressing. Serves 6 to 8.

Nutrition information per serving, 6 servings per recipe: Calories: 98. Protein: 3g. Total fat: 7.9g (sat. fat: 3.3g). Carbohydrates: 3g. Cholesterol: 17mg. Sodium: 500mg. Vitamin A: 10% DV. Vitamin C: 22% DV.

It may seem an unlikely pairing, but radishes and oranges are really a good combination. Try them together in this attractive green salad.

Romaine Lettuce with Oranges and Radishes

1 head Romaine lettuce, torn into bite-sized pieces
3 navel oranges, peeled, sliced crosswise, slices cut in half
½ cup thinly-sliced radishes
⅓ cup slivers of red onion
4 tablespoons roasted and salted sunflower seeds

Dressing:
3 tablespoons olive oil
2 tablespoons red wine vinegar
1 tablespoon finely chopped shallot
¼ teaspoon salt

Heap lettuce on a large platter. Arrange orange slices, radishes and red onions on top of lettuce. Right before serving, scatter on the sunflower seeds. Whisk together the dressing ingredients. Pour dressing on salad at the table and toss lightly. Serve immediately. Serves 6.

Nutrition information per serving, 6 servings per recipe: Calories: 204. Protein: 3g. Total fat: 14.2g (sat. fat: 1.8g). Carbohydrates: 17g. Cholesterol: 0mg. Sodium: 100mg. Vitamin A: 21% DV. Vitamin C: 89% DV.

NUTRITION INFORMATION PER **10** RADISHES, ¾" DIAMETER , RAW:

Calories: 7
Total fat: 0g
    (saturated fat: 0g)
Fiber: 1g
Sodium: 11mg
Potassium: 3% Daily Value
Vitamin A: 0% Daily Value
Vitamin C: 17% Daily Value
Iron: 1% Daily Value
Calcium: 1% Daily Value

RADISHES

SNAP PEAS

SNAP PEAS

SNAP PEAS are a type of edible pod pea, in which the pod grows tightly around the enclosed peas. Plump snap peas are distinctly different from their relative, snow peas, which are very flat. Peas are a legume with a history that predates the Great Pyramids. In ancient times they were used only in their dried form. It wasn't until the seventeenth century, when Louis XIV discovered the joys of fresh green peas, that *Pisum sativum* found new favor. Sugar snap peas are a hybrid that were refined in the 1970s by horticulturist Calvin Lamborn. They are actually a cross between English peas and snow peas. Snap peas are crunchy and sweet, and don't require shelling. Aren't we lucky that Calvin perfected them just in time for us?

HANDLING: Pods should be firm, plump, and glossy with no yellowing. Sugar snaps should snap crisply. Refrigerate peas soon after picking. The sugars that make them sweet and tasty convert to starches at room temperature. Store in a plastic bag in the refrigerator for no longer than a few days.

SIMPLE PREPARATION: Rinse before eating. Snap the stem end and pull down along the pod, removing the strings on both sides of the pod. Snap peas are delicious and sweet eaten raw. Add them to salads or serve as part of a vegetable platter. Very brief cooking brings out the brilliant green and sweetness of snap peas. Don't let these legumes linger more than a minute or two in the steamer. That's all they need—otherwise they will turn pale and soft. Light sautéeing or stir-frying is also an excellent way to prepare snap peas.

This quick-to-fix stir-fry is a great combination of colors, textures, and tastes. It is a complete meal served on top of hot orzo tossed with fresh parsley.

Snappy Snap Pea Stir-fry on a Bed of Parsley Orzo

1 tablespoon sesame oil
3 cloves garlic, finely minced
6 green onions, sliced in 1-inch pieces on the diagonal
½ teaspoon red chili pepper flakes
1 red bell pepper, cut into slivers
2 small yellow summer squash or golden zucchini, cut in slices ¼-inch thick
4 cups snap peas, left whole, with strings and tips removed
1 tablespoon soy sauce
plenty of freshly ground black pepper

Heat oil in a large skillet or wok over medium-high heat. Add garlic, green onions, and chili peppers. Stir-fry for 1 minute. Add bell pepper, summer squash, and snap peas. Stir-fry for 3 to 4 minutes longer or until vegetables are hot and just barely tender-crisp. If vegetables begin to stick add a splash of water, vegetable broth, or dry white wine to the pan. Season with soy sauce and black pepper. Serve immediately on a bed of Parsley Orzo. Serves 4.

Parsley Orzo

1 cup uncooked orzo
1 teaspoon butter
¼ cup finely chopped fresh parsley
¼ teaspoon salt

Bring a medium-sized pot of water to a boil. Cook orzo until just tender. Drain well. While still very hot, toss with butter. Sprinkle on the parsley and salt. Toss until well distributed. Serves 4.

Nutrition information per serving of Snap Pea Stir-fry on Parsley Orzo, 4 servings per recipe: Calories: 221. Protein: 8g. Total fat: 4.7g (sat. fat: 1.1g). Carbohydrates: 36g. Cholesterol: 2.5mg. Sodium: 306mg. Vitamin A: 28% DV. Vitamin C: 230% DV.

Snap peas don't really need much assistance if they are garden-fresh. Here is a little something you can do to make them just a bit more special.

Snap Peas with Shallots

   1 tablespoon butter
   1 large shallot, finely minced
   4 cups snap peas, left whole, with strings and tips removed
   ¼ teaspoon salt
   2 to 3 tablespoons vegetable broth or water

Heat butter in a large skillet over medium-low heat. Add the shallot and sauté 2 to 3 minutes. Add the peas, sprinkle with salt, and stir to coat with butter. Add liquid to the pan, cover, and cook for 3 or 4 minutes more or until peas are barely tender-crisp and still bright green. Serve immediately. Serves 4.

Nutrition information per serving, 4 servings per recipe: Calories: 101. Protein: 4g. Total fat: 3g (sat. fat: 1.8g). Carbohydrates: 14g. Cholesterol: 7.5mg. Sodium: 175mg. Vitamin A: 5% DV. Vitamin C: 147% DV.

NUTRITION INFORMATION PER ½ CUP SNAP PEAS, RAW:

Calories: 30
Total fat: <0.2g
    (saturated fat: 0g)
Fiber: 3.6g
Sodium: 3mg
Potassium: 4% Daily Value
Vitamin A: 1% Daily Value
Vitamin C: 72% Daily Value
Iron: 8% Daily Value
Calcium: 3% Daily Value

SNAP PEAS

SNOW PEAS

SNOW PEAS are the thin, flat parent of stubby snap peas. The exact origin of snow peas isn't known, although it is assumed to be in China. Snow peas were cultivated in Europe, where they have been eaten for centuries. Snow peas must be harvested while their inner peas are still tiny and have not yet begun to bulge out. Like snap peas, they are eaten pod and all. Snow peas and snap peas are in far greater demand than shelling peas. Only 5 percent of shelling peas make it to market fresh—the other 95 percent are canned or frozen. Too bad any pea finds its way into a can.

HANDLING: Snow peas are always somewhat soft and flexible, but they should be green and fresh-looking with a perky stem end. Store in a plastic bag in the refrigerator and use them soon after harvest. Like snap peas, their sugar content converts to starch during storage, and they will lose their bright, sweet flavor. Wash just before using. Break off the stem end and pull down along the side of the pod to remove the string. Snow peas usually have a thick string on only one side of the pod.

SIMPLE PREPARATION: Like snap peas, snow peas can be eaten raw. I think they are at their best very lightly stir-fried. A short trip in the wok or frying pan, with a little bit of peanut or sesame oil intensifies their flavor and color. A splash of soy sauce is the final touch.

Frozen cheese-filled pasta most often finds itself under marinara sauce. In this recipe you can enjoy tortellini in a completely different role.

Chinese Pasta Salad

8 ounces frozen cheese-filled tortellini or tortelloni*, cooked, rinsed in cool water, and drained
1 red or yellow bell pepper, cut in strips
1 green pepper, cut in strips
½ cup green onions, chopped
2 cups snow or snap peas, tips and strings removed, very lightly steamed

Dressing:
2 tablespoons olive or canola oil
1 teaspoon sesame oil
2 tablespoons rice vinegar
2 tablespoons reduced-sodium soy sauce
1 clove garlic, pressed or finely minced
1 teaspoon freshly grated ginger root
freshly ground black pepper to taste

Gently toss pasta with vegetables in a large bowl. Whisk dressing ingredients together until well blended. Pour over salad and toss to distribute dressing evenly. Cover and refrigerate salad for several hours to allow flavors to mesh. Toss again before serving. Serves 6.

*Tortellini and tortelloni are merely shapes of pasta. They are both a little ring of pasta with filling. Tortellini is smaller than tortelloni. My favorite brand is Putney Pasta, so named for its place of origin—Putney, Vermont. Putney Pastas are dependable, delicious, and creative frozen pastas. Available in natural food stores. A bit of a splurge, but well worth it.

Nutrition information per serving, 6 servings per recipe: Calories: 267. Protein: 12g. Total fat: 8g (sat. fat: 2.6g). Carbohydrates: 36g. Cholesterol: 40mg. Sodium: 617mg. Vitamin A: 14% DV. Vitamin C: 108% DV.

Flavors and textures are perfectly balanced in this delicious salad. Serve it as a side dish to accompany simply-prepared tofu. If you're lucky you'll have just enough left over to have for lunch the next day.

Chinese Cabbage and Snow Pea Salad

2 cups snow peas, tips and strings removed, cut in half on the diagonal
2 cups Chinese cabbage, cut into thin ribbons
1 medium carrot, cut into matchstick pieces
2 green onions, thinly sliced on the diagonal
¼ pound very thin pasta (capellini or spaghettini), broken in pieces, cooked, rinsed in cold water, and drained
freshly grated black pepper to taste
1 tablespoon toasted sesame seeds (for garnish)

Dressing:
3 tablespoons peanut oil
3 tablespoons rice vinegar
2 tablespoons reduced-sodium soy sauce
1 tablespoon Dijon mustard
2 cloves garlic, pressed or finely minced
1 tablespoon sugar or honey

Very lightly steam snow peas—they should still be crisp and bright green. Rinse under cold water and drain well. In a large bowl, combine peas, Chinese cabbage, carrot, green onions, and pasta. Whisk together the dressing ingredients and pour over vegetables and pasta. Season liberally with black pepper. Gently toss to distribute dressing evenly. Garnish with toasted sesame seeds. Serves 6 to 8.

Nutrition information per serving, 6 servings per recipe: Calories: 170. Protein: 4g. Total fat: 7.6g (sat. fat: 1.2g). Carbohydrates: 20g. Cholesterol: 0mg. Sodium: 293mg. Vitamin A: 44% DV. Vitamin C: 72% DV.

NUTRITION INFORMATION PER ½ CUP SNOW PEAS, COOKED:

Calories: 34
Total fat: <0.2g
    (saturated fat: 0g)
Fiber: 3.4g
Sodium: 3mg
Potassium: 5% Daily Value
Vitamin A: 1% Daily Value
Vitamin C: 63% Daily Value
Iron: 9% Daily Value
Calcium: 3% Daily Value

SORREL

SORREL

SORREL is a relative of rhubarb. If you've tasted *Rumex acetosa* or *R. scutatus,* this will come as no surprise. Sorrel derives its name from the old French *surele,* meaning sour. But sour shouldn't define sorrel's personality—there's so much to this perennial herb. Its delicate arrow-shaped leaves impart a lemony zest to salads. When cooked, sorrel transforms into a lively tasting purée that can be added to soups and sauces. Although not commonly used in this country, sorrel is a popular herb in France where it is regarded as a spring tonic. It is also used as the base for classic sorrel sauce and sorrel soup.

HANDLING: Sorrel has thin, delicate leaves that will only keep for several days. Store in a plastic bag in the refrigerator. If your sorrel comes in a bunch with a tight band, remove it along with any damaged leaves before storing. When ready to use, rinse in cool water, and spin or pat dry. Strip the leaves from their stems.

SIMPLE PREPARATION: Sorrel adds a wonderful tartness to salads. Roll or stack the leaves and cut crosswise with a sharp knife to create slivers of sorrel that can be sprinkled on a fresh green salad. Or use the slivers as a garnish for cream soups. Sorrel can also be cooked. Use it as you would fresh spinach, alone or in combination with chard or other tender greens. With simple simmering, fresh sorrel leaves will be reduced to a velvety purée that can be used to flavor sauces, soups, or quiches—sorrel has a natural affinity for eggs. If you don't plan to use your sorrel right away, the purée can be frozen. Avoid cooking highly acidic sorrel in aluminum or cast-iron cookware.

This is a potato salad that makes a statement. It is filled with ingredients that aren't at all modest—Greek olives, Feta cheese, tangy sorrel leaves, and earthy lentils, all dressed with a sharp vinaigrette. It is truly irresistible.

Lentil Potato Salad with Sorrel

1 cup dried lentils
1 bay leaf
1 small onion, finely chopped
¾ teaspoon salt
1 pound small new potatoes or fingerling potatoes
3 stalks celery, finely chopped
¼ cup finely chopped red onion
⅓ cup sliced Kalamata olives
½ cup Feta cheese, crumbled
1 cup finely shredded sorrel leaves
freshly ground black pepper

Dressing:
4 tablespoons olive oil
1 tablespoon balsamic vinegar
2 tablespoons freshly-squeezed lemon juice
2 garlic cloves, minced or pressed
1 tablespoon Dijon mustard

Place lentils, bay leaf, onion, and ¼ teaspoon of the salt in a medium-sized saucepan and cover with approximately 3 cups of water. Bring to a boil, reduce heat, and simmer until lentils are just tender but not falling apart—approximately 30 minutes. Remove from heat, and drain lentils in a colander. Remove the bay leaf. While the lentils are cooking, put on the potatoes to cook. Boil whole, unpeeled potatoes until just tender but not falling apart. Drain, and cut into 1-inch cubes. When lentils and potatoes have cooled to room temperature, carefully toss them together with the celery, red onion, olives, Feta cheese, sorrel leaves, the remaining ½ teaspoon salt, and plenty of freshly ground black pepper. Whisk together the dressing ingredients. Pour over the potato salad and toss to distribute evenly. Serve at room temperature or chilled. Serves 8.

Nutrition information per serving, 8 servings per recipe: Calories: 232. Protein: 7g. Total fat: 11.3g (sat. fat: 3.3g). Carbohydrates: 25g. Cholesterol: 12.5mg. Sodium: 496mg. Vitamin A: 60% DV. Vitamin C: 44% DV.

Here is a delicate sauce that can be used to transform simple vegetables into an elegant dish. Drizzle on top of lightly steamed asparagus, fresh green beans, or cauliflower florets. The cream is optional—it adds yet another dimension to this wonderful sauce.

Simple Sorrel Sauce

1 tablespoon butter
1 small shallot, finely minced
2 cups sorrel leaves, stems removed, chopped coarsely
1 to 2 tablespoons white wine
½ teaspoon salt
freshly ground white pepper
¼ to ⅓ cup cream or half and half (optional)

Heat butter in a medium-sized saucepan over medium-low heat. Add shallots. Sauté until the shallots are just about tender. Add the sorrel, white wine, and salt. Simmer for 4 to 5 minutes, or until sorrel is completely soft and almost sauce-like. Add pepper to taste. The sauce can be served as is, or pureed in a food processor or blender with the cream. Makes ½ to ¾ cup of sauce—just enough to dress up vegetables for 4.

Nutrition information per serving, 4 servings per recipe, prepared without cream: Calories: 39. Protein: <1g. Total fat: 2.8g (sat. fat: 1.8g). Carbohydrates: 3g. Cholesterol: 7.5mg. Sodium: 331mg. Vitamin A: 58% DV. Vitamin C: 25% DV.

NUTRITION INFORMATION PER ½ CUP SORREL, COOKED:

Calories: 19
Total fat: 0.2g
    (saturated fat: 0g)
Fiber: 0.7g
Sodium: 3mg
Potassium: 6% Daily Value
Vitamin A: 220% Daily Value
Vitamin C: 92% Daily Value
Iron: 5% Daily Value
Calcium: 6% Daily Value

SORREL

SPINACH

SPINACH has no similarity to the gray-green "vegetable" in a can we were made to eat as children. Spinach is tender, delicate, and full of life. The very best spinach is locally grown —commercial spinach is bred to be thicker and sturdier to withstand the rigors of travel. Spinach has its roots in Persia, where it was cultivated for the enjoyment of exotic long-haired cats (lucky felines!). Centuries later, in 1806, spinach made its debut in seed catalogs in the United States. There are three types of spinach: savoy with its crinkly leaves, flat or smooth-leaf, and popular semisavoy. Although spinach is often cited as a good source of calcium and iron, these minerals are not absorbed well from spinach because of the presence of oxalic acid.

HANDLING: Spinach leaves should be green and fresh-looking, and free of yellow-tinged or wilty leaves. Store your spinach loosely in a plastic bag in the refrigerator, where it will keep for several days. Don't wash spinach until you're ready to use it. And when you're ready to wash it, be sure to devote enough time to this simple task to do a thorough job. The curly leaves of spinach can harbor dirt and grit. The most wonderfully prepared recipe will be ruined by the crunch of grit. Wash spinach more than once by filling a sink with cool water and dunking the spinach leaves until no more dirt appears in the sink after draining. Pat or spin spinach dry. Thick or tough stems should be removed.

SIMPLE PREPARATION: Young, tender spinach leaves make the finest salad. With the addition of red onion, croutons, and a simple vinaigrette, you will have a true celebration of spring. Spinach leaves are also great on sandwiches as a flavorful substitute for lettuce. Spinach can also be cooked to create wonderful pizza and pasta toppings, and to add to casseroles and quiches. Or just lightly sauté spinach for a quick side dish. Heat a small amount of olive oil in a large skillet, add 1 or 2 cloves minced or pressed garlic, and sauté lightly until slightly golden. Add spinach and stir until wilted, approximately 3 minutes. Since spinach is 80 to 90 percent water, fresh spinach dramatically reduces in volume during cooking. Two to three pounds of spinach will yield approximately 2 cups cooked!

Here is spinach at its finest. This gorgeous salad combines the rich, deep taste of spinach with red onion, Feta cheese, and garden-fresh tomatoes, intensified by a drizzle of warm vinaigrette. Truly an outstanding salad!

Spinach Salad with Warm Vinaigrette

1 pound fresh spinach leaves
½ cup red onion, cut in slivers
a combination of red cherry tomatoes and small yellow plum tomatoes—1 pint total
1 cup Feta cheese, cut in ½-inch cubes

Dressing:
4 tablespoons olive oil
2 tablespoons red wine vinegar
1 teaspoon Dijon mustard
¼ teaspoon salt

plenty of freshly ground black pepper
1½ cups plain croutons

Rinse spinach thoroughly. Trim off thick or tough stems. Spin or pat dry. If leaves are small, leave whole. Tear larger leaves in half. Place spinach in salad bowl or on a very large platter. Scatter red onions, tomatoes, and Feta cheese cubes on top. Whisk together the dressing ingredients in a small saucepan and heat over medium heat until just hot. Drizzle hot dressing evenly over the salad. Grind on black pepper, top with croutons, and serve immediately. Serves 8.

Nutrition information per serving, 8 servings per recipe: Calories: 187. Protein: 6g. Total fat: 13.3g (sat. fat: 5.8g). Carbohydrates: 9g. Cholesterol: 26mg. Sodium: 528mg. Vitamin A: 52% DV. Vitamin C: 42% DV.

This is a beautiful and tasty spinach dish. Hot from the oven the frittata is puffed and golden. It falls slightly after a minute or two, but is still quite impressive looking—and so delicious.

Spinach Leek Frittata

1 tablespoon butter
3 leeks, thinly sliced
1 large bunch fresh spinach, approximately ¾ pound, washed and chopped
1 tablespoon fresh oregano, minced (or 1 teaspoon dried)
3 eggs, beaten
1½ cups lowfat milk
4 ounces Gruyere cheese (or other Swiss), grated
½ teaspoon salt
lots of freshly ground black pepper
2 cups fresh bread cubes, cut into ¼-inch cubes (French or Italian bread is best)

Preheat oven to 350°F. Melt butter in a large, heavy skillet over medium heat. Add the leeks and sauté for 2 to 3 minutes. Add the spinach and oregano and cook until just wilted, about 1 minute. Remove from heat and set aside. Beat the eggs, milk, cheese, salt, and pepper together. Stir in the bread cubes and spinach-leek mixture. Mix well. Pour into an oiled 9½-inch baking dish or cast-iron skillet. Bake for approximately 40 minutes or until golden and firm. Serves 6.

Nutrition information per serving, 6 servings per recipe: Calories: 224. Protein: 14g. Total fat: 10.2g (sat. fat: 5.6g). Carbohydrates: 18g. Cholesterol: 109mg. Sodium: 420mg. Vitamin A: 59% DV. Vitamin C: 40% DV.

This quick-to-prepare recipe is great as a pasta topping or broiled on pieces of French bread. It is also wonderful as a pizza topping, either on your own homemade crust, foccacia, or filo dough crust.

Fresh Spinach and Feta Topping

¾ pound fresh spinach leaves
¼ cup green onions, chopped
¼ cup fresh parsley, chopped
¼ cup fresh basil, chopped
1 cup Feta cheese, crumbled
⅓ cup Greek olives, pitted and chopped

Rinse spinach thoroughly. Trim off thick or tough stems. Drop clean spinach into boiling water and cook until just wilted. Drain, squeeze out excess liquid, and chop. Mix spinach with remaining topping ingredients. Serve or use immediately.

Nutrition information per serving, 4 servings per recipe: Calories: 177. Protein: 10g. Total fat: 11.7g (sat. fat: 8.3g). Carbohydrates: 6g. Cholesterol: 50mg. Sodium: 778mg. Vitamin A: 81% DV. Vitamin C: 53% DV.

NUTRITION INFORMATION PER ½ CUP SPINACH, RAW:

Calories: 6
Total fat: 0g
    (saturated fat: 0g)
Fiber: 1.1g
Sodium: 22mg
Potassium: 4% Daily Value
Vitamin A: 9% Daily Value
Vitamin C: 13% Daily Value
Iron: 4% Daily Value
Calcium: 3% Daily Value

BUTTERNUT SQUASH is one of my favorites. I respect its versatile and predictable personality. Like most winter squashes, it is also very patient. A member of the Cucurbit family, squashes are really edible gourds. Unlike perishable summer squashes that are harvested when immature, winter squashes mature on the vine and will store for quite a long time. Butternut squash is a particularly good keeper. Butternuts are elongated, tan-colored squashes, with a bulbous end that encloses the seeds, and a neck that is solid flesh. The skin of butternut is smooth and relatively thin, making it easy to peel. The flesh is deep orange with a mild taste. Butternut squash is at home in burritos and stir-fry, and is also perfect as the squash in "pumpkin" pie.

HANDLING: Here is a vegetable with few demands. Like all winter squashes, butternuts keep best in a cool place—ideally, at 50° to 55°F, with low humidity. They will store for months under ideal conditions. Butternut squash will also keep in the warmth of your kitchen, but not for as long a time.

SIMPLE PREPARATION: To easily handle butternut squash, cut the entire neck off just above the bulbous seed cavity. Snap or cut off the hard stem. Now your two pieces can more easily be cut lengthwise. Scoop out seeds with a metal spoon (no seeds in the neck!). If you'll be baking the squash, just put the large pieces, with their skins, in a covered baking dish. Add ¼ to ½ cup of water to the bottom of the baking dish to help steam the squash. Cover and bake in a 350°F oven until tender, approximately 40 to 60 minutes, depending on the size of your pieces. If you'll be cutting the squash up to be used in a recipe that calls for peeled squash, use a carrot peeler. Cubes of butternut squash can be sautéed in a small amount of canola or olive oil and seasoned with salt and pepper. You'll need to use some liquid to help steam the squash tender— apple juice adds a nice touch of sweetness. After lightly browning the cubes in oil, add liquid and cover. Cook until tender, approximately 15 to 20 minutes, adding more liquid as necessary.

This recipe was given to me by John Thompson, sous chef at the Free State Brewery in Lawrence, Kansas. Thanks to John for taking the time to write it out, and to Chuck Magerl, proprietor, for letting us share it. It is a celebration of Kansas produce—and sunflowers!

Sunflower Stir-fry

Sauce:
1 tablespoon shredded fresh ginger root
¼ cup dry sherry
¼ cup of your favorite soy sauce (more or less can be used, according to your tastes)

Stir fry:
1½ tablespoons sesame oil (or any other oil you like)
one small butternut squash, peeled, seeded, and cut into 1 x ½ x ⅛-inch pieces
another 2 cups of an assortment of any of the following vegetables:
    broccoli florets
    julienne carrots
    sliced leeks
    sliced red or yellow onion
    sliced zucchini and/or yellow squash
    julienne daikon
    sliced broccoli rabe
    cauliflower florets
    julienne bell peppers
    sliced shiitake mushrooms
    sliced portobello mushrooms
    snow peas or sugar snap peas
¼ to ½ cup hulled, roasted, unsalted sunflower seeds

Combine sauce ingredients and simmer 10 minutes to infuse the flavors, or multiply the recipe and simply mix and store in a pour bottle. To prepare, heat a wok or sauté pan, add oil, add vegetables and stir-fry until all vegetables are just hot and crisp. Then add the sunflower seeds, the sauce, and toss. Season to taste with black pepper (you won't need any salt) and serve over your favorite rice (mine is Thai jasmine). Serves 4 to 6.

Nutrition information per serving, 4 servings per recipe, using reduced-sodium soy sauce: Calories: 208. Protein: 5g. Total fat: 10.5g (sat. fat: 1.3g). Carbohydrates: 18g. Cholesterol: 0mg. Sodium: 616mg. Vitamin A: 124% DV. Vitamin C: 51% DV.

Black bean burritos are a staple at our house—quick to make and so satisfying to eat. In this recipe, black beans are combined with butternut squash, and accented by cumin and cinnamon to create burritos that will fill your kitchen with the wonderful smells of fall.

Savory Butternut & Black Bean Burritos

1 tablespoon canola oil
½ medium-sized onion, chopped
3 cups peeled butternut squash, cut into ½-inch cubes
½ teaspoon ground cumin
¼ teaspoon cinnamon
½ teaspoon salt
2 cups cooked black beans, drained and rinsed
8 flour tortillas
1½ cups grated reduced-fat Monterey jack or Cheddar cheese
light sour cream, fresh cilantro, and salsa for garnish

Heat oil in heavy skillet over medium heat. Add onions and sauté for 5 minutes. Add winter squash cubes and continue to cook over medium heat, stirring often until squash is just tender. If your mixture begins to stick, add a little water (or apple juice) to help steam the squash. When squash is just tender, add cumin, cinnamon, and salt. Stir carefully to distribute spices. Add the beans and heat through. Preheat oven to 350°F. You're now ready to assemble the burritos. In a large oblong baking dish (not oiled) lay out one tortilla. Place ⅛ of the bean mixture down the center, top with 3 tablespoons of cheese and roll up tightly. Continue to do this with remaining ingredients, lining up your burritos in the pan as you go. Bake uncovered for approximately 15 to 20 minutes until burritos are heated through. Serve burritos topped with a dollop of sour cream and a sprinkling of chopped fresh cilantro, with salsa on the side. Makes 8 burritos—enough for 8 polite adults, 6 hungry adults, or 4 teenage boys.

Nutrition information per serving, 8 servings per recipe: Calories: 322. Protein: 14g. Total fat: 12g (sat. fat: 5.1g). Carbohydrates: 39g. Cholesterol: 23mg. Sodium: 473mg. Vitamin A: 60% DV. Vitamin C: 20% DV.

Although we're always experimenting with new recipes at our house, there are those we return to again and again. This is one of those recipes—dependable, and always satisfying.

Baked Winter Squash with Apples

1½ pounds uncooked winter squash, peeled and cut into cubes
½ pound fresh cranberries (optional)
2 to 3 apples, chopped
¼ cup raisins
juice and grated peel of 1 small orange
1¼ tablespoons maple syrup (or honey)
dash each of salt and cinnamon

Preheat oven to 350°F. Combine squash, cranberries, apples, and raisins in a small buttered casserole dish. Mix juice, orange peel, maple syrup, and salt together. Pour over squash mixture. Lightly dust with cinnamon, cover, and bake until squash is tender, approximately 30 to 45 minutes. Serves 4.

Nutrition information per serving, 4 servings per recipe: Calories: 199. Protein: 2g. Total fat: <1g (sat. fat: <1g). Carbohydrates: 47g. Cholesterol: 0mg. Sodium: 76mg. Vitamin A: 120% DV. Vitamin C: 78% DV.

NUTRITION INFORMATION PER ½ CUP BUTTERNUT SQUASH, COOKED:

Calories: 41
Total fat: 0g
　　　(saturated fat: 0g)
Fiber: 3g
Sodium: 4mg
Potassium: 8% Daily Value
Vitamin A: 71% Daily Value
Vitamin C: 25% Daily Value
Iron: 3% Daily Value
Calcium: 4% Daily Value

WINTER SQUASH

WINTER SQUASH, like acorn squash, spaghetti squash, and sweet

dumpling, all have distinct personalities. Like butternut squash, they are mature members of the Cucurbit family. Unlike butternut, they have a thicker skin and are usually not peeled before cooking. Acorn squash is most familiar—a small, deeply-ribbed squash with dark-green, glossy skin. Inside the flesh is pale yellow and somewhat flaky and dry. Acorns are probably the most popular squash for stuffing. Spaghetti squash is a large, smooth-skinned, pale yellow or ivory oblong squash. Its nondescript exterior belies its novel interior—strands of golden, crisp-tender vegetable "spaghetti." It's definitely not the most versatile of squashes, but spaghetti squash ranks high in the fun department . . . and it is delicious. The exact origin of this unusual squash is still left to speculation. Sweet dumplings are just what their name implies—small and sweet. Most sweet dumplings are about the size of a large apple and weigh under a pound—just about a single serving size. Inside is a tender pale yellow to orange colored flesh, best baked and savored plain, or packed with your favorite stuffing.

HANDLING: Acorn squash is generally a good keeper but it should be eaten within three months of harvest. Like butternut, it is best stored in cool and dry conditions. Spaghetti squash and sweet dumpling squash also prefer cool (not cold, no refrigeration please), dry storage conditions, but neither of these winter squashes will keep as long as acorn or butternut. It's best to use them within several weeks after harvesting.

SIMPLE PREPARATION: Acorn squash is excellent cut in half and baked until tender. Cutting through the hard shell requires a sharp knife and a steady hand. Cut in half lengthwise, scoop out the seeds and fibers, and then place cut side down in a covered baking pan with enough water to barely cover the bottom of the pan. Bake in a 350°F oven until tender, approximately 45 minutes or until shell is easily pierced with a fork. When acorn squash is sweet, it really needs very little embellishment. If you prefer, or if the squash isn't the most flavorful, turn the baked halves over and brush with butter and a drizzle of maple syrup. Bake for a few minutes longer to allow the flavors to penetrate the squash. Spaghetti squash needn't be a challenge to prepare. The easiest way to cook this large and tough-skinned squash is to boil it whole. It is a rather unusual sight to see a whole squash bobbing around in a pot of water, but I don't believe there is a more simple way to cook it. You will need a large enough pot to hold the spaghetti squash. Boil until a fork easily pierces the outer shell. Depending on the size of the squash this will take anywhere from 25 to 45 minutes. Remove from the pot. When cool enough to handle, slice in half lengthwise (now a very easy task), carefully scoop out the seeds, and rake out the strands of "spaghetti" with a fork. Toss with olive oil or butter, grated Parmesan cheese if you'd like, and salt and pepper. Or serve with your favorite pasta sauce. Cold strands of spaghetti squash can also be used to make a delicious cold salad—follow the directions for your favorite pasta salad. Sweet dumplings are best just baked or steamed. Cut the little squashes in half, remove seeds, and bake like acorn squash until tender. Or place in a steamer basket and steam until tender. How long they take to cook will depend on their size, but generally these small squashes will take about half the time of acorn squash. Sweet dumplings can be baked whole by cutting a small "lid" out of the top (like you do with a jack-o'-lantern) and scooping out the insides. Then add a small dab of butter, salt and pepper, and replace the lid. Bake until tender in a covered baking dish with a small amount of water added to help steam the squash. Be creative and stuff these little individual serving-sized squashes with a rice and vegetable mixture, or a combination of orzo, Feta, and herbs. Add seasoned tempeh to the stuffing for a one-dish meal. Return to the oven to heat through.

Winter squashes with big cavities, like acorn, practically ask to be stuffed. In this version, acorn squash is baked tender, then heaped with savory stuffing. Each stuffed half will serve two people. Cut the stuffed squash in half lengthwise and serve up an impressive-looking wedge of golden squash supporting a moist and delicious herbed stuffing. Serve with homemade cranberry relish or applesauce, and a pan of lightly sautéed greens—a fall feast.

Baked Acorn Squash with Herbed Stuffing

1 medium to large-sized acorn squash
1 tablespoon olive oil
1 clove garlic, minced finely
1 medium-sized onion, chopped
2 stalks celery, chopped
1 small apple, finely chopped
2 to 3 cups whole wheat bread cubes, cut in ½-inch cubes
½ cup vegetable broth
¾ teaspoon salt
freshly ground black pepper
1 tablespoon finely chopped fresh sage leaves (or 1 teaspoon dried)
1 teaspoon finely minced fresh rosemary (or ¼ teaspoon dried)
1 sprig fresh thyme leaves, finely chopped (or ¼ teaspoon dried)
2 tablespoons chopped fresh parsley

Preheat oven to 350°F. Cut each squash in half lengthwise. Scoop out the seeds. Place squash halves, cut side down, in a covered baking dish. Add several tablespoons of water to the dish, and bake until tender, approximately 40 minutes. Remove from oven, allow to cool slightly. Carefully scoop the pulp out into a small bowl, leaving about ¼ inch of flesh in the shell. Place the empty shells cavity-side up in a clean baking dish. Set aside. Heat the olive oil in a large skillet over medium heat. Add the garlic, onion, celery, and apple. Sauté until just tender, approximately 10 minutes. If vegetables begin to stick, add several tablespoons of water to the pan. Add bread cubes and toss with vegetables. Pour vegetable broth over the mixture, stirring to evenly distribute. Add the cooked squash, breaking up any large chunks. Finally, stir in the salt, pepper, and fresh herbs. Mix well. Remove stuffing from heat. Heap the filling into the squash shells. Cover, and return to oven for another 20 minutes or until heated through. Each half can be cut in half lengthwise. Serves 4.

Variations and Additions: When you're adding the herbs to the stuffing, throw in a handful of chopped pecans. Or try adding the chopped apple at the end of the stuffing preparation instead of sautéing it with the other vegetables—it will add texture to the stuffing.

Nutrition information per serving, 4 servings per recipe: Calories: 180. Protein: 4g. Total fat: 4.2g (sat. fat: <1g). Carbohydrates: 31g. Cholesterol: 0mg. Sodium: 543mg. Vitamin A: 10% DV. Vitamin C: 31% DV.

This is a wonderfully light dish. Serve it with a crisp green salad, a baguette (or two), and plenty of freshly grated Parmesan to go on top.

Spaghetti Squash with Fresh Tomatoes, Basil, and Mozzarella

1 medium-sized spaghetti squash
2 tablespoons olive oil
3 cloves garlic, finely minced
1 medium-sized shallot, minced
6 or 7 plum tomatoes, peeled and chopped
⅓ cup sun-dried tomatoes, cut in strips, soaked in 1 cup boiling water, drained
¾ teaspoon salt
freshly ground black pepper to taste
⅓ cup fresh basil leaves, finely shredded
6 ounces fresh Mozzarella, cut into ½-inch cubes
a handful of whole basil leaves for garnish

Put on the spaghetti squash to boil. When it is done, remove it from the pan and allow it to cool while you prepare the sauce. Heat the olive oil in a deep skillet over medium heat. Add the garlic and shallot. Sauté for 2 minutes. Stir in the fresh tomatoes (be careful—they tend to splatter when you add them). Also add the dried tomatoes, salt, and pepper. Cook for 3 to 4 minutes, stirring often. Remove from heat, stir in the shredded basil. Now go back to your cooked spaghetti squash, which should be cool enough to handle. Cut it open, scoop out the seeds, and carefully rake the strands into a large bowl. Add the Mozzarella cubes and toss. Cover, and allow to sit for several minutes so that the Mozzarella cubes can soften and begin to melt. Heap spaghetti squash onto a large, deep platter. Pour the hot sauce over all. Garnish with fresh, whole basil leaves. Serve immediately. Serves 6.

Nutrition information per serving, 6 servings per recipe: Calories: 172. Protein: 8g. Total fat: 8.7g (sat. fat: 3.5g). Carbohydrates: 13g. Cholesterol: 16mg. Sodium: 427mg. Vitamin A: 17% DV. Vitamin C: 37% DV.

NUTRITION INFORMATION PER ½ CUP SQUASH, COOKED:

SPAGHETTI SQUASH	ACORN SQUASH
Calories: 23	Calories: 57
Total fat: <0.3g	Total fat: <0.2g
(saturated fat: <0.2g)	(saturated fat: 0g)
Fiber: 2.2g	Fiber: 3g
Sodium: 14mg	Sodium: 4mg
Potassium: 3% Daily Value	Potassium: 13% Daily Value
Vitamin A: <1% Daily Value	Vitamin A: 4% Daily Value
Vitamin C: 5% Daily Value	Vitamin C: 18% Daily Value
Iron: 2% Daily Value	Iron: 6% Daily Value
Calcium: 2% Daily Value	Calcium: 5% Daily Value

WINTER SQUASH

SUMMER SQUASH

SUMMER SQUASH is really a gourd that is harvested at an immature stage

so that its skin and seeds are still edible. Cucurbitaceae pepo come to us in a variety of shapes, sizes, and colors. There are the long, slender zucchini, yellow straightneck, and yellow crookneck squashes. Although traditionally green, one zucchini variety is a rich, deep gold with accents of green—a feast for the eyes as well as the palate. Patty pan are small, squat, disc-shaped squash with a scalloped edge. Patty pan are usually creamy ivory or deep yellow. Less common, but worth a mention, is chayote, a pear-shaped summer squash with a single, central seed. Chayote is commonly used in Mexican cooking. Although not widely available in all parts of the United States, it is popular in the South and Southwest. Squash is a native American food that has grown alongside beans and corn for thousands of years.

HANDLING: Summer squash is approximately 95 percent water. This means it begins to dehydrate (and shrivel) if not used within several days of harvest. Always choose firm, solid, and small summer squash—this is definitely *not* a vegetable where bigger is better. If you have an excessive amount of summer squash (this can easily happen if you have a garden), you'll need to find ways to use your bounty. One of the best ways to preserve zucchini is to transform it into delicious cakes and breads, which can easily be frozen.

SIMPLE PREPARATION: Young, tender summer squash can be eaten raw. Wash carefully, then cut into thin matchstick pieces to top off a green salad—particularly attractive if you have both green and gold squash. Cooking summer squash is quick. Slice squash and lightly sauté in olive oil. Add a splash of soy sauce and cook over medium heat, stirring often. Cook until lightly golden and barely tender. Sprinkle with Parmesan or toss with snips of fresh basil. If you have garden-fresh tomatoes, peel, cut in chunks, and throw them in with the squash just at the end of the cooking time. You can also steam or boil summer squash, but pay careful attention—there isn't much good to be said about mushy, overcooked summer squash. Summer squash is a nice addition to stir-fried vegetables and is wonderful in quiches.

Enchiladas take a bit of work to prepare. One bite reminds me of why they are worth the effort.

Zucchini and Cheese Enchiladas

2 tablespoons butter
4 tablespoons unbleached white flour
1 teaspoon chili powder
½ teaspoon ground cumin
2 cups skim milk
2 cups grated reduced-fat sharp Cheddar cheese
½ teaspoon salt
black pepper to taste
1 tablespoon canola oil
1½ cups chopped onion
4 garlic cloves, minced or pressed
1 large bell pepper, chopped (sweet red pepper is attractive)
6 cups chopped zucchini
chopped hot peppers (optional)
16 to18 corn tortillas
2 cups chopped tomatoes

In a saucepan, melt the butter over medium heat. Stir in the flour, chili powder, and cumin to make a thick paste. Add the milk a little at a time, using a wire whisk. Slowly add the cheese, stirring constantly until cheese is melted. Season with salt and pepper. Remove from heat and set aside. Preheat oven to 400°F. Heat oil in a large skillet over medium heat. Add the onions and garlic and sauté for 5 minutes. Add bell pepper and zucchini (and chopped hot peppers if you're using them) and sauté 2 more minutes. Add ¼ cup of water, cover, and steam veggies until tender. Remove vegetables from heat, and drain excess liquid. Gently mix in ⅔ of the cheese sauce. Lightly oil a 9 x 13-inch baking dish. To assemble, place two tortillas side by side at one end of the pan (they will probably overlap slightly in the middle). Spread a generous amount of filling down the center of the tortillas, then fold them over and roll up the tortillas. Place filled enchiladas seam-side-down in the pan. Continue in this manner until you have filled the pan. Spoon remaining sauce on top and garnish with tomatoes. Bake, uncovered, for 20 to 25 minutes. Serves 8.

Nutrition information per serving, 8 servings per recipe: Calories: 325. Protein: 16g. Total fat: 12.3g (sat. fat: 5.3g). Carbohydrates: 36g. Cholesterol: 29mg. Sodium: 406mg. Vitamin A: 26% DV. Vitamin C: 58% DV.

We have a small garden that always includes several zucchini plants. When the first shiny little zuke appears, we go into the garden to admire its beauty. The next day we go into the garden and discover that there are at least fifteen zucchinis ready to pick, and half of them are the size of a large rolling pin . . . or so it seems. For the next two months, one of our vegetable drawers becomes the zucchini holding tank. Where this all leads me is to zucchini cake. When we have sautéed, quiched, stuffed, and eaten all the zucchini we can bear, there is still one way to prepare this prolific summer vegetable that we never tire of—baked into a spicy, moist cake.

Chocolate Spice Zucchini Cake

½ cup canola oil
½ cup honey
½ cup turbinado or brown sugar
2 eggs, beaten
½ cup buttermilk
2 teaspoons vanilla extract
1¾ cups whole wheat pastry flour, unbleached white flour, or a combination
⅓ cup cocoa powder
1 teaspoon baking powder
½ teaspoon baking soda
1½ teaspoons cinnamon
¼ teaspoon ground cloves
¼ teaspoon ground ginger
½ teaspoon salt
2 teaspoons finely-grated orange rind
1½ cups finely-grated zucchini

Preheat oven to 350°F. Oil a 7½ x 12-inch baking pan. In a large bowl, combine oil, honey, and sugar. Mix in eggs, buttermilk, and vanilla extract. Sift together the flour, cocoa, baking powder, baking soda, cinnamon, cloves, ginger, and salt. Add to the wet mixture. Mix well. Stir in the orange rind and zucchini. If your batter seems too thin, add just a little bit more flour. Pour batter into prepared pan and bake for approximately 45 minutes or until firm to the touch. Serves 12.

Nutrition information per serving, 12 servings per recipe: Calories: 235. Protein: 5g. Total fat: 10.2g (sat. fat: 1.3g). Carbohydrates: 31g. Cholesterol: 28mg. Sodium: 183mg. Vitamin A: 3% DV. Vitamin C: 4% DV.

This light soup is easy to prepare and perfect for a summer meal. Serve it with thick slices of dark, moist bread.

Summer Chowder

1 tablespoon canola oil
1 large onion, chopped
1 cup chopped celery
2 to 3 small zucchini or yellow squash, sliced in ½-inch-thick slices, then cut in half
1 large potato, cubed
2 tablespoons flour
3 cups water or stock
1 bay leaf
½ teaspoon salt
1 cup corn kernels, fresh or frozen
2 tablespoons chopped fresh parsley
⅛ teaspoon grated nutmeg
scant ¼ teaspoon crushed thyme
¼ teaspoon ground cumin
1 cup lowfat milk
1 cup grated reduced-fat Cheddar cheese
black pepper to taste

Heat oil in soup pot over medium heat. Add onion, celery, squash, and potato and sauté for 5 minutes. Sprinkle flour over vegetables and stir until lightly coated. Add water or stock to pot along with bay leaf and salt. Bring to a boil, lower heat to simmer, and cook, covered, until vegetables are tender, approximately 15 minutes. Add the corn, parsley, nutmeg, thyme, and cumin. Simmer 5 to 10 more minutes. Slowly add the milk, then cheese, stirring constantly until cheese is melted. Season liberally with black pepper and serve at once. Serves 6.

Nutrition information per serving, 6 servings per recipe: Calories: 167. Protein: 8g. Total fat: 6.2g (sat. fat: 2.3g). Carbohydrates: 19g. Cholesterol: 14mg. Sodium: 331mg. Vitamin A: 9% DV. Vitamin C: 25% DV.

NUTRITION INFORMATION PER ½ CUP SUMMER SQUASH, COOKED:

Calories: 18
Total fat: <0.2g
   (saturated fat: 0g)
Fiber: 1.4g
Sodium: 1mg
Potassium: 5% Daily Value
Vitamin A: 3% Daily Value
Vitamin C: 8% Daily Value
Iron: 2% Daily Value
Calcium: 2% Daily Value

SUMMER SQUASH

SWEET POTATOES

SWEET POTATOES are not yams. Sweet potatoes are a member of the

morning glory family, a family with gorgeous trailing vines. The potatoes are the roots. Yams are actually a starchy tropical vegetable almost never seen in this country—a technicality, I suppose, but also an important point of clarification to an often-asked question. Sweet potatoes are generally divided into two categories. There are the drier, more starchy, less-sweet varieties, such as Jersey. These sweet potatoes are more slender and have a firmer flesh. And there are the more moist, sweet, and softer varieties, commonly called "yams." These sweet potatoes tend to be more round. There are many varieties of sweet potatoes, in a range of colors and sizes. You'll just have to sample lots of them to appreciate the subtle differences in taste and texture.

HANDLING: When sweet potatoes are first dug up, their skins are very fragile. If you scrub them vigorously, you might be surprised that their skin rubs off. Before storing, the potatoes should be cured. Spread them out in a warm, humid spot for about a week. For most cooks this may seem like an irrelevant piece of information, but if you get your sweet potatoes fresh from the grower or at a farmers' market, curing greatly improves their flavor. Once they are cured sweet potatoes can be stored like winter squashes, in a cool, dry place. Don't refrigerate sweet potatoes unless they're cooked. Sweet potatoes don't like cold temperatures and will spoil quickly if chilled.

SIMPLE PREPARATION: Treat sweet potatoes the same as you would baking potatoes—scrub and bake. This is really the best way to enjoy their natural sweetness. Bake in a 400°F oven until tender, approximately 45 minutes for larger sweet potatoes. Cooked sweet potatoes can be peeled and mashed for use in a number of recipes. Sweet potato pie, made just like pumpkin pie, is rich and creamy. Leftover cooked sweet potatoes can be added to waffles, pancakes, breads, cookies, and muffins to add moist sweetness and boost vitamin A content.

Sweet potato vines are beautiful. When the rest of the garden is played out in the fall, the dark-green trailing vines still hug the ground, densely covering the soil where the sweet potatoes wait to be dug. The sweet potatoes come inside about the same time I do—when the days are often rainy and the nights have a chill. This is soup weather. Sweet potatoes make a rich, thick soup with the taste and color of fall.

Creamy Sweet Potato Soup

    1 tablespoon butter
    1 large onion, chopped
    4 cups vegetable broth
    4 cups chopped, peeled sweet potatoes
    2 tart apples, peeled and chopped
    4 or 5 roma tomatoes, peeled and chopped
    ¾ teaspoon salt
    freshly ground black pepper to taste
    the leaves from 1 sprig of fresh thyme (or ¼ teaspoon dried thyme)
    1 cup lowfat milk

Heat butter in a soup pot over medium-low heat. Add onion and sauté until soft, approximately 8 to 10 minutes. Add a little of the broth if the onions begin to stick. Add the sweet potatoes and apples and stir for a minute or two. Add the tomatoes, the remaining broth, salt, pepper, and thyme. Increase heat to medium-high and bring to a boil. Reduce heat to medium-low and simmer, covered, until vegetables are tender—35 to 45 minutes. For a perfectly creamy soup, puree in a food processor or blender, working in small batches. Take care not to burn yourself when pureeing the hot soup. If you would like your soup to have more texture, blend just a portion of the soup. Return pureed soup to pot and gently heat while you slowly stir in the milk. When heated through, ladle into bowls and serve at once. Serves 6 to 8.

Nutrition information per serving, 6 servings per recipe: Calories: 341. Protein: 6g. Total fat: 3.2g (sat. fat: 1.8g). Carbohydrates: 71g. Cholesterol: 8mg. Sodium: 394mg. Vitamin A: 395% DV. Vitamin C: 90% DV.

If you end up with leftover cooked sweet potato, you have just the excuse you need to make homemade biscuits. These slightly-sweet biscuits are a beautiful golden color.

Sweet Potato Biscuits

2 cups flour (a combination of whole wheat pastry and unbleached white is great)
1 tablespoon baking powder
½ teaspoon salt
4 tablespoons cold butter
1 cup skim milk
1 cup mashed or pureed sweet potatoes
1 tablespoon maple syrup or honey

Preheat oven to 425°F. Sift the flour, baking powder, and salt into a medium-sized bowl. Cut the butter into the flour mixture using a pastry cutter or two knives—the mixture should look like coarse meal. Mix together the milk, sweet potatoes, and maple syrup or honey. Pour into the flour mixture and stir with a fork until the mixture just comes together. Turn dough out onto a floured surface and knead, using a light touch, until the dough is fairly smooth. Use a little more flour if the dough is too sticky, remembering that short and gentle kneading will give you the most tender biscuit. Pat the dough out to a thickness of ¾ to 1 inch. Cut with a 2-inch biscuit cutter. Place on a lightly oiled cookie sheet. Bake 15 minutes, or until just golden. Serve hot! Makes approximately 20 biscuits.

Nutrition information per biscuit: Calories: 85. Protein: 2g. Total fat: 2.4g (sat. fat: 1.5g). Carbohydrates: 14g. Cholesterol: 6mg. Sodium: 149mg. Vitamin A: 30% DV. Vitamin C: 5% DV.

If you want to dress your sweet potatoes up just a bit, and make your kitchen smell warm and inviting, this is the classic combination to do it.

Sweet Potato and Apple Bake

2 or 3 medium-sized sweet potatoes, peeled and sliced approximately ¼-inch thick
2 flavorful fall apples, peeled and sliced approximately ¼-inch thick
1 tablespoon butter
¼ cup maple syrup or honey
¼ cup apple cider
½ teaspoon salt

Preheat oven to 350°F. Oil a large shallow baking dish. Arrange sweet potato and apple slices attractively in dish. Combine butter, maple syrup or honey, cider, and salt in a small saucepan over low heat. Stir until butter is melted. Pour half of the mixture over the sweet potatoes and apples. Bake for approximately 45 minutes or until sweet potatoes are tender. Halfway through the baking, drizzle the remaining butter/syrup mixture over the sweet potatoes and apples. Serves 6.

Nutrition information per serving, 6 servings per recipe: Calories: 264. Protein: 2g. Total fat: 2.2g (sat. fat: 1.3g). Carbohydrates: 58g. Cholesterol: 5mg. Sodium: 219mg. Vitamin A: 281% DV. Vitamin C: 51% DV.

NUTRITION INFORMATION PER 1 MEDIUM SWEET POTATO, COOKED:

Calories: 118
Total fat: 0g
    (saturated fat: 0g)
Fiber: 4.4g
Sodium: 12mg
Potassium: 11% Daily Value
Vitamin A: 249% Daily Value
Vitamin C: 47% Daily Value
Iron: 3% Daily Value
Calcium: 3% Daily Value

SWEET POTATOES

TOMATOES

TOMATOES

TOMATOES deserve a book of their own—and many have been written about this member of the nightshade family. Tomatoes, *Lycopersicon esculentum,* are botanically a fruit but are considered a vegetable by rule of the Supreme Court of the United States in 1893. Seems there was a tariff dispute that had to do with an importer trying to get by without paying import tax on his tomato "fruit." For the sake of import tax, tomatoes then became a vegetable. There are thousands of tomato varieties falling into one of three general categories—full-sized slicing tomatoes, cherry tomatoes, and plum or Italian tomatoes. Colors abound, with bright reds, oranges, yellows, bi-coloreds, yellow-whites, and purples. If you need a reason to get up early on Saturday morning for the farmers' market, tomatoes are it. It's just not possible to pick a juicy, vine ripened tomato and ship it 2,000 miles to put on your dinner table.

HANDLING: With great care. If it's good and ripe, it needs to be eaten soon. Bring it home nestled carefully in the top of your shopping bag. If tomatoes are still slightly green or hard, allow to sit out at room temperature—they will continue to ripen. Refrigerate tomatoes only if they are fully ripe and you want to stop the ripening process. Before using refrigerated tomatoes, allow them to warm back to room temperature.

SIMPLE PREPARATION: Bite into a vine-ripened tomato still warm from the sun—this is the finest garden taste of all. Toss thick tomato slices with a little olive oil, balsamic vinegar, and some fresh basil. Or spread goat cheese on a slice of Italian bread and top with a slab of tomato and a dab of pesto—broil if you'd like. Homemade pizza is the best with tomato slices instead of heavy sauces. If you're using fresh tomatoes in cooked dishes you probably will want to peel them. Submerge whole tomatoes in boiling water for approximately 10 seconds. Remove and plunge them into cold water. When the tomatoes are cool enough to handle, just slip the skins off. Remove the core. If you want to also remove the seeds, cut the tomato in half lengthwise. Squeeze gently over a bowl. The seeds and gelatinous substance around them will come right out, leaving the meat of the tomato.

Pasta e fagioli is a classic Italian pasta and bean dish. This hearty version uses lots of summer produce combined with cannellini beans (white kidney beans), penne pasta, and a variety of herbs. Serve with freshly grated Parmesan, a crisp green salad, and lots of chewy Italian bread—a perfect company meal!

Pasta e Fagioli

2 tablespoons olive oil
4 to 6 cloves of garlic, pressed or minced
1 large onion, chopped
2 medium carrots, diced
3 stalks celery, chopped
1 green or red bell pepper, chopped
1 medium zucchini, chopped (regular green zucchini or beautiful golden zucchini)
¼ cup chopped fresh parsley
1 tablespoon fresh oregano, minced (or 1 teaspoon dried)
2 tablespoons fresh basil, minced (or 1 teaspoon dried)
¼ teaspoon dried summer savory
1 bay leaf
1½ to 2 cups cooked cannellini beans, rinsed and drained (or 15 ounce can)
3 cups chopped, peeled tomatoes (plum tomatoes are the best)
½ cup dry white wine
1 teaspoon salt
½ pound penne pasta (or other tube shape)
plenty of freshly ground black pepper
chopped fresh parsley for garnish

Heat oil in a large, deep skillet over medium heat. Add the garlic, onions, carrots, and celery. Sauté for 3 to 4 minutes. Add the bell pepper and zucchini. Continue to sauté 2 to 3 minutes longer. Toss in the herbs and stir to distribute well. Gently stir in the beans, tomatoes, wine, and salt. Bring to a boil, reduce heat to medium-low, and allow to simmer for 20 minutes. While beans and vegetables are cooking, put on a large pot of water and cook the pasta until just tender but still firm. Drain well. Toss pasta and vegetables together and season with plenty of black pepper. Mound on a large, deep platter. Garnish with chopped parsley. Serve immediately. Serves 6 to 8.

Nutrition information per serving, 6 servings per recipe: Calories: 234. Protein: 8g. Total fat: 4.8g (sat. fat: <1g). Carbohydrates: 36g. Cholesterol: 0mg. Sodium: 396mg. Vitamin A: 81% DV. Vitamin C: 73% DV.

Gazpacho is the ultimate summer food—cold, refreshing, and easy to make. It should be made with really excellent garden-fresh tomatoes. This version includes cannellini beans, which make this cold soup a real meal.

Great Gazpacho

4 large tomatoes, diced
½ cup minced red onion
1 medium-sized cucumber, peeled, seeded, and diced
1 medium-sized green bell pepper, diced
1 medium-sized yellow bell pepper, diced
1 hot pepper, seeds removed, minced (optional)
2 cloves garlic, minced
⅓ cup minced fresh parsley
2½ cups tomato juice or tomato-based vegetable juice
juice of 1 lemon
2 tablespoons red wine vinegar
1 tablespoon olive oil
1 tablespoon honey or other sweetener
½ teaspoon salt
freshly ground black pepper to taste
1½ cups cannellini beans, cooked, rinsed, drained

You don't need a blender or food processor to make gazpacho. It is wonderful prepared by hand—full of little chunks of fresh vegetables. Just mix all ingredients together in a large bowl. Refrigerate for several hours. Stir again before serving. If you prefer a finer texture, you can certainly use a machine. Of course, you'll want to leave the beans out until everything else has been blended. Another option is to blend half your veggies (tomatoes, onion, cuke, peppers, garlic, and 1 cup of the tomato juice) to create a thick base, then add the rest of the chopped veggies, seasonings, and beans. Serves 6 to 8.

Nutrition information per serving, 6 servings per recipe: Calories: 143. Protein: 5g. Total fat: 2.4g (sat. fat: <1g). Carbohydrates: 25g. Cholesterol: 0mg. Sodium: 555mg. Vitamin A: 25% DV. Vitamin C: 141% DV.

You don't need to fuss much with a really good tomato. But if you want something just a little dressed-up, here is a very delicious and adaptable recipe. It's best to serve this dish at room temperature.

Herbed Garden-Fresh Tomatoes

6 to 8 ripe tomatoes, thickly sliced or chopped in large chunks
4 tablespoons finely minced onion
2 to 4 tablespoons fresh basil, minced
½ teaspoon dried dill weed
4 tablespoons fresh parsley, chopped
¼ teaspoon salt
freshly ground black pepper
2 tablespoons olive oil
2 tablespoons balsamic vinegar

Place tomato pieces and onion in a bowl. Sprinkle herbs, salt, and pepper over tomatoes and toss very gently to distribute. Whisk together the olive oil and vinegar. Drizzle over tomatoes and once again toss gently. Delicious served at once, at room temperature. This dish can be chilled, but it is best served within several hours of preparation. Serves 6.

Variations and additions: Slivers of green pepper; slices of cucumber; lightly steamed green beans; slices or chunks of ripe avocado; crumbles of Feta cheese and a small handful of Greek olives; leave out the dill weed and add a sprinkle of fresh cilantro and a splash of lime juice.

Nutrition information per serving, 6 servings per recipe: Calories: 72. Protein: 1g. Total fat: 4.4g (sat. fat: <1g). Carbohydrates: 6g. Cholesterol: 0mg. Sodium: 102mg. Vitamin A: 18% DV. Vitamin C: 48% DV.

NUTRITION INFORMATION PER MEDIUM TOMATO, RAW:

Calories: 24
Total fat: <0.2g
    (saturated fat: 0g)
Fiber: 1.8g
Sodium: 10mg
Potassium: 7% Daily Value
Vitamin A: 14% Daily Value
Vitamin C: 37% Daily Value
Iron: 3% Daily Value
Calcium: 1% Daily Value

TOMATOES

GREEN TOMATOES are vine-ripened tomatoes cut short on time in the

fall. The nights were just too cool and the days too short to grow into what they were supposed to become. But green tomatoes shouldn't be left on the vine to go to waste. They can be carefully stored to slowly ripen, offering memories of summer well into the fall. I remember one Thanksgiving, carefully unwrapping a red tomato from our summer garden. It wasn't as good as an August tomato, but it was definitely a tomato to be proud of. But green tomatoes aren't just a red tomato wannabe. Green tomatoes are a firm, tart, fall treat, and an excuse to make fried green tomatoes.

HANDLING: If you want your green tomatoes to slowly ripen, you will need to handle them carefully and be attentive to them. They should be stored in a cool spot, between 55° and 60°F, away from direct light. Some gardeners suggest storing tomatoes on a rack, not touching each other, covered with newspaper. Some people unearth whole plants with tomatoes and hang them upside down in an attic to store. My best success in storing green tomatoes was achieved by wrapping individual tomatoes in newspaper and storing them in a cool area. Whatever your method, you will need to constantly check on the tomatoes, "harvesting" the ripe ones, and culling the ones that begin to rot. If you want to more quickly ripen green tomatoes, put them in a paper bag or a plastic container with a punctured lid—the tomatoes put off ethylene gas that helps to ripen the fruit when it is placed in a closed container. If you intend to use your tomatoes green, keep them off that sunny windowsill, and use them soon.

SIMPLE PREPARATION: Green tomatoes are tart and firm, more like a green apple than a red, juicy tomato. They are good finely chopped in salsas and chutneys, but the classic recipe is fried green tomatoes. There are many variations on this southern specialty, but the basic recipe is simple. Dip thick slices of green tomatoes in seasoned cornmeal, flour, or bread crumbs and sauté in oil until golden brown. Best when eaten at the Whistlestop Cafe.

Green tomatoes are perfect in pies and crisps, especially when combined with apples and raisins. Enjoy this special fall crisp—the wonderful aroma of it baking is worth the effort alone!

Green Tomato and Apple Crisp

4 cups chopped green tomatoes
4 cups peeled, sliced apples
½ cup golden raisins
1 teaspoon grated orange rind
2 tablespoons unbleached white flour
½ teaspoon cinnamon
¼ teaspoon ground cloves
⅛ teaspoon salt
½ cup honey

Crisp Topping:

½ cup whole wheat pastry flour
½ cup brown or turbinado sugar
1 cup quick-cooking rolled oats
1 teaspoon cinnamon
¼ teaspoon nutmeg
¼ teaspoon salt
⅓ cup cold butter

Preheat oven to 350°F. In a large bowl, combine the tomatoes, apples, raisins, and orange rind. Sprinkle on the unbleached white flour, cinnamon, cloves, and salt, and toss with apples. Drizzle on the honey. Mix to distribute honey evenly. Place fruit in an oiled 7½ x 12-inch baking dish. Combine flour, sugar, rolled oats, cinnamon, nutmeg, and salt in a medium-sized bowl. Cut in the butter with a pastry cutter or two knives until the mixture is the texture of coarse meal. Spread topping over the apple mixture. Bake for approximately 50 minutes, or until apples are tender. Serves 8.

Nutrition information per serving, 8 servings per recipe: Calories: 323. Protein: 4g. Total fat: 8.4g (sat. fat: 4.9g). Carbohydrates: 57g. Cholesterol: 20mg. Sodium: 196mg. Vitamin A: 14% DV. Vitamin C: 55% DV.

Around October in Kansas, gardeners prepare for the first hard frost. There are usually a number of false alarms before the real killing frost finally falls on gardens and puts them to rest for the season. Sweet potatoes must be dug, herbs harvested, and those beautiful green tomatoes must be saved. Some green tomatoes will sit on a windowsill to slowly ripen, others will be stored to enjoy later, and others will simply be used for what they are—firm, flavorful, somewhat tart vegetables (fruits) that make wonderful pasta sauce.

Green Tomato Pasta Sauce over Fettuccini

1 pound fettuccini
6 tablespoons olive oil
6 garlic cloves, finely minced
½ of a hot pepper, finely minced or ¼ teaspoon chili pepper flakes (optional)
1 pound green tomatoes, very finely chopped (4 to 5 medium-sized tomatoes)
⅓ cup sun-dried tomatoes, soaked in boiling water for 10 minutes, drained, cut in slivers
¼ cup fresh basil leaves, shredded
¼ cup finely minced parsley
¾ teaspoon salt
black pepper to taste

Put on a large pot of water and cook the pasta while you prepare the sauce. Heat oil in a large, deep skillet over medium heat. Add garlic and hot pepper (if using) and sauté for 1 minute. Carefully add the green tomatoes (be prepared—they may splatter) and dried tomatoes. Continue to cook, stirring often for 3 to 5 minutes longer. Drain pasta and return to cooking pot. Pour hot sauce over pasta and add the basil and parsley. Season with salt and pepper. Toss to combine well. Serve immediately. Top with plenty of freshly grated Parmesan cheese. Serves 8.

Nutrition information per serving, 8 servings per recipe: Calories: 477. Protein: 17g. Total fat: 12.4g (sat. fat: 2.3g). Carbohydrates: 74g. Cholesterol: 210mg. Sodium: 244mg. Vitamin A: 11% DV. Vitamin C: 28% DV.

NUTRITION INFORMATION PER 1 MEDIUM GREEN TOMATO, RAW:

Calories: 30
Total fat: <0.2g
  (saturated fat: 0g)
Fiber: 1.8g
Sodium: 16mg
Potassium: 7% Daily Value
Vitamin A: 8% Daily Value
Vitamin C: 48% Daily Value
Iron: 3% Daily Value
Calcium: 2% Daily Value

TOMATOES

TURNIPS

TURNIPS

are another of those vegetables that produce two different crops—the round roots and the sturdy green tops. Unless you purchase turnips locally you won't often see the two parts of the turnip united. This member of the Brassicaceae or mustard family has its origins in the colder climates of Russia, Siberia, and Scandinavia. Of the many varieties of turnips grown, the small purple-tinged variety are the most common. Rutabagas are the much larger orange and purple roots, and are actually a different botanical species of turnip. Rutabagas are also called "Swede turnips", partially because of their popularity in Sweden (smart folks!).

HANDLING: Turnips should be firm and smooth. Purple-topped white turnips should be a modest size—no larger than 2 or 3 inches in diameter. Rutabagas are larger and have a rougher look. They should be solid and heavy. If your turnips come with the tops attached, separate them before storage. The greens should be dark and fresh-looking. Treat as you would any other perishable leafy vegetable—store loosely in a plastic bag in the refrigerator, don't wash them until you're ready to use them. Consume within a few days of purchase. Turnip roots will keep in the vegetable drawer of the refrigerator for about a week. Since turnips have a high water content, they will begin to lose water and shrivel if they are stored too long. Rutabagas are more fleshy and dense. They will store better—two weeks or longer in the refrigerator.

SIMPLE PREPARATION: Tender young turnips are delicious raw. When they are fresh and small they don't even need to be peeled. Slice or sliver them in salads or on vegetable platters. Turnips can also be used in stir-fry—adding a nice crunch and a perky flavor. When turnips and rutabagas are grown under the right conditions and are purchased fresh, they will be flavorful and sweet. They are excellent prepared simply. If the turnips are large (always in the case of rutabagas) you will need to peel them. Cut into uniform cubes. Steam until tender. Rutabagas are especially good mashed. Turnips and rutabagas can also be baked in the oven. Place cubes in a baking pan, add slices of carrots, onions, and potatoes, and a drizzle of olive oil. Season with salt and pepper. Cover with foil. Bake in a 350°F oven until tender, approximately 45 minutes.

When slow-simmered in a soup or stew, root vegetables and onions develop a wonderfully-mellow, almost-sweet taste, especially when the recipe is prepared with good, homemade stock. Serve this cool-weather stew over a scoop of brown rice, accompanied by hot Sweet Potato Biscuits. For dessert—Green Tomato and Apple Crisp. The perfect autumn feast!

Root Stew

    2 tablespoons olive oil
    4 cloves garlic, finely minced
    1 large onion, chopped
    3 medium-sized turnips with their greens (peel and chop roots in ½-inch cubes, coarsely
        chop the greens)
    1 medium-sized rutabaga, peeled and chopped in ½-inch cubes
    2 medium-sized potatoes, chopped in ½-inch cubes
    2 carrots, cut in ½-inch chunks
    4 to 6 cups vegetable stock or water*
    5 tablespoons reduced-sodium soy sauce
    1 bay leaf
    freshly ground black pepper to taste

Heat oil in a large soup pot over medium heat. Add garlic and onion. Sauté for 3 to 5 minutes. Add all ingredients except the turnip greens. Bring to a boil, reduce heat to medium-low, and simmer uncovered for 25 minutes. Add turnip greens and continue to simmer until vegetables are tender, approximately 15 minutes longer. Serves 6.

*How much liquid you use depends on how thick you want your stew. You may want it so thick you can almost eat it with a fork. Or you may prefer to have lots of broth for dipping biscuits or bread. Both ways are most wonderful!

Nutrition information per serving, 6 servings per recipe: Calories 148. Protein: 3g. Total fat: 4.3g (sat. fat: <1g). Carbohydrates: 23g. Cholesterol: 0mg. Sodium: 558mg. Vitamin A: 78% DV. Vitamin C: 63% DV.

The best part of this recipe is the wonderful fragrance of simmering apples and turnips, with a hint of cinnamon. This very mild, and naturally sweet preparation of turnips is an excellent way to introduce this root to those who might think of turnips as a strong-tasting vegetable. Serve as a side dish with black beans and brown rice, accompanied by hot cornbread just out of the oven.

Simple Skillet Turnips and Apples

1 tablespoon canola oil
½ cup chopped onion
1 medium apple, chopped (approximately ¾ cup)
3 cups chopped turnips or rutabagas (½-inch cubes)
½ cup fresh apple cider or apple juice
1 small cinnamon stick
¼ teaspoon salt

Heat oil in a large skillet over medium heat. Add onion and sauté for 3 to 5 minutes. Add apple and sauté 2 more minutes. Add turnips, cider or juice, cinnamon stick, and salt. Cover and reduce heat to medium-low. Stir occasionally, and add more liquid if necessary to prevent sticking. Simmer until turnips are tender, approximately 20 minutes. Remove cinnamon stick before serving. Serves 4.

Nutrition information per serving, 4 servings per recipe: Calories 84. Protein: 1g. Total fat: 3.3g (sat. fat: <1g). Carbohydrates: 13g. Cholesterol: 0mg. Sodium: 193mg. Vitamin A: 0% DV. Vitamin C: 27% DV.

NUTRITION INFORMATION PER ½ CUP TURNIPS, COOKED:

Calories: 14
Total fat: 0g
   (saturated fat: 0g)
Fiber: 1.7g
Sodium: 39mg
Potassium: 3% Daily Value
Vitamin A: 0% Daily Value
Vitamin C: 15% Daily Value
Iron: 1% Daily Value
Calcium: 2% Daily Value

TURNIPS

About some of the ingredients ◆ ◆ ◆

THERE is usually a large container of olive oil on my kitchen counter and a bottle of balsamic vinegar in the cupboard. Among the glass jars filled with grains and beans, orzo and basmati rice are staples. The freezer holds a stack of quart containers marked "vegetable broth". Sun-dried tomatoes, tofu, canola oil, whole wheat pastry flour . . . these ingredients find their way into quite a few of the *Rolling Prairie* recipes. Although the stars of these recipes are definitely fruits, vegetables, and herbs, you will need to stop by the grocery store for a few other supplies. Here is a quick guide to some of the most often used ingredients.

Asiago cheese: A hard Italian cheese, good for grating. Asiago is similar to Parmesan, but a bit more pungent. Freshly grated hard cheeses are superior in taste and texture to powdery pre-grated cheeses. A good hand-held cheese grater is a relatively small investment (usually under $15.00) that will make this job fun!

Balsamic vinegar: A mixture of red wine vinegar and the juice of grapes that has been aged in wooden casks. Balsamic vinegar has a wonderful deep, mellow flavor and rich color. Excellent in salad dressings and as a condiment to splash on vegetables.

Barley: Chewy, easily digestible grain, delicious in soups, stews, and as the base for cold salads. Rinse 1 cup barley in cold water. Drain. Add to 3 cups water in a saucepan. Bring to a full boil. Reduce to simmer, cover. Cook until tender—about 1 hour. Yield: approximately 3½ cups.

Basmati rice: An aromatic, long-grain rice with a unique nutty flavor. Named after the basmati flower of Asia. Basmati rice comes in both white and brown varieties. Rinse rice well in cool water. Drain. Place one cup rice and two cups water in a medium-sized saucepan. Bring to a full boil, reduce heat to simmer, cover, and cook (undisturbed) until water is absorbed. White basmati takes approximately 15 minutes to cook, brown basmati takes about 45 minutes. When preparing rice to be used in a cold salad, or for any recipe where you want the grains to be separate, sauté rinsed rice briefly in a small amount of oil before adding water to the pan. Stir often to ensure all the individual grains are lightly coated with oil.

Canola oil: A mild-tasting cooking oil, made from rape seed. It's roots are Canadian, and hence it's name: <u>Can</u>adian <u>o</u>il, low-<u>ac</u>id. Canola oil is high in monounsaturated fats. It's best to buy oil that is packaged in glass. Keep your canola oil refrigerated.

Chèvre cheese: The generic French name for cheese made from goat's milk. In recipes calling for chèvre, use one of the mild, soft, cream-cheese varieties like *Montrachet*.

Feta cheese: Salty, porous white cheese packed in brine, traditionally made from goat's or sheep's milk. Feta is also made with cow's milk. It is wonderful in green salads, tossed with pasta, or added to cold potato or pasta salads. A little of this extremely flavor-packed cheese will enliven any dish.

Ginger root: Pale brown, compact root that is extremely flavorful, and full of "hot" ginger taste. Peel the thin skin with a paring knife and finely grate. A small amount goes a long way. Especially good combined with soy sauce and garlic in marinades.

Gruyere cheese: Aged and somewhat dry Swiss cheese with few or no holes! Gruyere has a wonderful deep flavor—excellent in quiches.

Honey: One of the few locally produced sweeteners. Usually available at the farmers' market. The flavor varies greatly depending on where the bees did their gathering work. Get to know a beekeeper and learn more about the subtleties and advantages of honey.

Lemon zest: Just the very outer skin of the lemon. When grating citrus skin, be careful not to dig into the bitter, white pithy part under the colored skin.

Olive oil: An excellent oil for salad dressings, and general kitchen use in any recipe where its distinctive flavor will be welcomed. The best quality olive oil is extra-virgin. Virgin olive oil is made from lower grade olives or may be from a second pressing but is still a fine product. Flavors vary greatly—experiment with brands, varieties and countries of origin. Olive oils from Greece are usually full flavored. Oils from Italy, especially the brilliant green ones, tend to be more fruity, while others offer a delicate, mellow taste. There are also a number of fine California olive oils. Organic olive oils are available. Store your oil away from heat and light, preferably in a dark glass container.

Orzo: Rice-shaped pasta. Boil orzo in water the way you would any pasta. Drain well. Orzo is a nice light pasta—a fine addition to soups, or as the base of a pasta salad. Traditionally made with white flour, it is also available in whole wheat.

Parmesan cheese: Aged hard cheese with a nutty, salty taste. True Parmesan comes from the region around Parma, Italy and is marked "Parmigiano-Reggiano". Many fine Parmesans are available from other areas of Italy, as well as some notable American Parmesans, which are softer and more salty. Fine organic Parmesan is also available.

Rice Vinegar: Slightly sweet vinegar distilled from rice. Rice vinegar is excellent combined with soy sauce, garlic, and ginger for marinating tofu or for pasta salads with an Oriental personality.

Salt: For most of my cooking (not baking) I use Vege-Sal, an all purpose vegetized seasoning salt. It definitely still contributes sodium, but since it is more flavorful than plain salt, I generally end up using less. For baking I use sea salt, not because I feel it is more nutritious, but because I don't care for all the additives in regular salt that keep it free-flowing and white.

Seitan: High protein "wheat meat" is made from gluten—the principal protein in wheat. Seitan can be found in the refrigerated case at natural food stores and Oriental markets. It is often packaged in seasoned liquid which can be added to stews and soups. Seitan is excellent in stir-fry.

Shallots: A small, mild onion with brown skin. Shallots contribute a gentle taste—especially good in homemade salad dressings where the taste of garlic or regular onion would be too much.

Soy Sauce: This term refers broadly to the salty, brown, liquid condiment made from soybeans. There is a world of difference between the more traditionally fermented shoyu and tamari, and the caramel-colored liquid often sold as soy sauce. Read the label. True soy sauce should say "traditionally brewed" or "naturally brewed" on the label. The ingredients also tell the story. Shoyu is made from water, soybeans, wheat and salt. Tamari is wheat-free. Try both— their flavors are rich and distinct. Many organic brands are available, also reduced-sodium versions.

Sun-dried tomatoes: Flavorful, concentrated, dried tomatoes—it takes seventeen pounds of fresh tomatoes to make one pound of dried tomatoes. To soften, pour boiling water over tomatoes and let sit for five minutes. Most tomatoes aren't actually "sun-dried", although it's a lovely concept. Sonoma produces fine organic dried tomatoes.

Tofu: Also called bean curd, tofu is a high protein food made from soybeans. The beans are cooked and pressed. A coagulant is added to the liquid (soymilk) from the beans which causes the milk to separate into curds and whey. The curds are pressed into cakes—voila, tofu! Versatile, easy to digest, readily available in most grocery stores. Look in the produce or dairy department for fresh tofu made from organically grown beans.

Turbinado sugar: Pale brown-colored sugar that has been steam-cleaned but not chemically-whitened. In recipes where I want a texture I can't achieve with liquid sweeteners such as honey or maple syrup, I use turbinado sugar. Available in natural food stores, as is certified organic sugar—moist, pale-colored, and excellent in any recipe calling for turbinado or brown sugar.

Unbleached white flour: Creamy-colored white flour that hasn't gone through the chemical bleaching process. Unbleached flour is nice to use when you want to achieve a lighter product, like delicately flavored foccacia. Look for certified organic flour.

Vegetable broth: There are a number of powdered vegetable broths, but none can come close to homemade. Make a big pot of it when you have the time, and freeze quarts of it to have on hand whenever you need it. I make mine in the biggest soup pot I have using distilled water, chunks of organic carrot, onion, celery, shiitake mushrooms, and several bay leaves. I simmer this brew for an hour or so, then strain off and discard the vegetables. There are endless variations on homemade broth. You will need to experiment with a variety of vegetables. The smell of broth simmering is wonderful!

Whole wheat pastry flour: Whole wheat flour made from soft wheat, producing lighter, more tender wholegrain cakes, cookies, and biscuits. Pastry flour is not really appropriate for bread baking because of its lower gluten content. Available in natural food stores. Store wholegrain flour in a cool spot, ideally in an airtight container in the refrigerator if you're not going to use it soon. Look for certified organic flour.

About the Nutritional Analysis . . .

APPROACHES to diet abound. Just when we think we have a handle on how we should eat, another piece of seemingly contradictory nutrition information grabs the headlines. Pasta is good, too much pasta is bad. Eat margarine. No, eat butter. Cut down on fat, protein, and carbohydrates. What's left to eat?

THE truth is—there is no simple answer to the question of what is the best way to eat. Eating healthfully can't be reduced to a formula. Choosing the foods we eat is a multi-faceted process. We should be thinking about the source of our food. And by whose hands it has been prepared. Sound nutrition needs to enter into the picture. Fat, protein, carbohydrates—are they somewhat in balance? Are the foods we're eating fresh and full of life, with vitamins and minerals still intact? *Rolling Prairie Cookbook* can't begin to tackle all these complicated questions. What this cookbook can do is provide a nutritional analysis of each recipe. This gives you a tool to work with. If you're watching your fat intake, or limiting sodium, or monitoring cholesterol, you have an idea of what these recipes bring to the table nutritionally. You can make adjustments to recipes so that they work for you. Although it is a temptation to say "salt to taste" in the recipes, I deliberately use exact amounts. This way, you're not left to the whim of the salt shaker, not knowing how much sodium you've just added to that pot of soup, or bowl of salad.

SO where does the nutritional analysis for each recipe come from? Recipe ingredients are individually coded and entered into the DINE System computer program. The DINE program calculates major nutrients per serving based on this information. Although the DINE calculations are accurate, I also want to say that these numbers aren't absolutes. The nutritional values for food are variable. The vitamin C content of a piece of fruit, for example, is affected by so many factors: the particular variety of the fruit, growing conditions, handling, exact size. These recipe analyses are meant to provide a reference point. I hope this information is helpful.

BIBLIOGRAPHY

Atlas, Nava. *American Harvest*. New Paltz, NY.: Amberwood Press, 1991.

Ballantyne, Janet. *Joy of Gardening Cookbook*. Pownal, Vt.: Storey Communications, Inc., 1984.

Braue, John Rahn. *Uncle John's Bread Book*. New York: Pyramid Communications, Inc., 1974.

Brody, Jane. *Good Food Book*. New York: W. W. Norton and Co., 1985.

Callan, Ginny. *Horn of the Moon Cookbook*. New York: Harper and Row, Publishers, Inc., 1987.

Creasy, Rosalind. *Cooking from the Garden*. San Francisco: Sierra Club Books, 1988.

Dennison, Drs. Darwin and Kathryn. *The Dine System: The Best Ever Activity and Food Record Book*. Amherst, New York: DINE Systems, Inc., 1990.

DeWitt, Dave, Mary Jane Wilan, and Mellisa T. Stock. *Hot and Spicy and Meatless*. Rocklin, Ca.: Prima Publishing, 1994.

Dille, Carolyn, and Susan Belsinger. *Herbs in the Kitchen*. Loveland, Co.: Interweave Press Inc., 1992.

Dooley, Barbara. *Peppers Hot and Sweet*. Pownal, Vt.: Storey Communications, Inc., 1990.

Finn, Jane Adams. "Beyond Baking Sweet Potatoes." *Taunton's Kitchen Garden,* January 1998, pp. 38–39.

Fletcher, Janet. *Fresh From the Farmers' Market*. San Francisco, Ca.: Chronicle Books, 1997.

Goldbeck, Nikki and David. *Nikki and David Goldbeck's American Wholefoods Cuisine*. New York: New American Library, 1983.

Greene, Bert. *Greene On Greens*. New York: Workman Publishing Company, Inc., 1984.

Guthrie, Helen A. *Introductory Nutrition*. St. Louis, Mo.: Times Mirror / Mosby College Publishing, 1989.

Hagen, Rolfe. "Sage Advice." *Taunton's Kitchen Garden,* July 1997, pp. 28–32.

Henry, Linda, and Heidi Kaisand. *Better Homes and Gardens Farmer's Market Cookbook*. Des Moines, Ia.: Better Homes and Gardens Books, 1993.

BIBLIOGRAPHY

Hewitt, Jean. *The New York Times Natural Foods Cookbook.* New York: Avon Books, 1972.

Hirsch, David. *The Moosewood Restaurant Kitchen Garden.* New York: Simon and Schuster, Inc., 1992.

Johnny's Selected Seeds Catalog. Albion, ME., 1998.

Katzen, Molly. *Moosewood Cookbook.* Berkeley, Ca.: Ten Speed Press, 1977.

_____. *Vegetable Heaven.* New York: Hyperion, 1997.

Killeen, Johanne, and George Germon. "Four Courses in Italian." *Taunton's Fine Cooking,* August/September 1994, pp. 34–39.

Kirchner, Bharti. "Delicious Indian Chaat." *Taunton's Fine Cooking,* June/July 1995, pp. 64–67.

Kraus, Sibella. *Greens: a Country Garden Cookbook.* San Francisco: Collins Publishers, 1993.

Lively, Ruth. "Cooking Tames Sage's Flavor." *Taunton's Kitchen Garden,* July 1997, pp. 32–34.

Madison, Deborah, and Edward Espe Brown. *The Greens Cookbook.* New York: Bantam Books, 1987.

Majure, Janet. *Recipes Worth Sharing.* Lawrence, Ks.: Breadbasket Publishing Company, 1997.

Margen, Sheldon, M.D. *The Wellness Encyclopedia of Food and Nutrition.* New York: Rebus / Health Letter Associates, 1992.

Moosewood Collective. *Moosewood Restaurant Book of Desserts.* New York: Clarkson N. Potter, Inc., 1997.

_____. *Moosewood Restaurant Cooks at Home.* New York: Simon and Schuster / Fireside, 1994.

_____. *Moosewood Restaurant Low-Fat Favorites.* New York: Clarkson Potter Publishers, Inc., 1996.

_____. *Sundays at Moosewood Restaurant.* New York: Simon and Schuster / Fireside, 1990.

Morash, Marian. *The Victory Garden Cookbook.* New York: Alfred A Knopf, Inc., 1982.

O'Connor, Nancy. *In the Bag: Recipes Prepared for the Rolling Prairie Farmers Alliance.* Lawrence, Ks.: Spring Wheat Nutrition Education Services, 1995.

_____. *In the Bag: Recipes Prepared for the Rolling Prairie Farmers Alliance.* Lawrence, Ks.: Spring Wheat Nutrition Education Services, 1996.

Onstad, Dianne. *Whole Foods Companion.* White River Junction, Vt.: Chelsea Green Publishing Company, 1996.

Petusevsky, Steven. "Great Greens." *Taunton's Fine Cooking,* February/March 1995, pp. 32–35.

Piper, Marjorie Ray. *Sunset Mexican Cookbook.* Menlo Park, Ca.: Lane Magazine and Book Company, 1969.

Rombauer, Irma, and Marion Rombauer Becker. *Joy of Cooking.* New York: The New American Library, 1964.

Rupp, Rebecca. *Blue Corn and Square Tomatoes.* Pownal, Vt.: Storey Communications, Inc., 1987.

Schardt, David. "Phytochemicals: Plants Against Cancer." *Nutrition Action Healthletter,* April 1994, pp. 1, 9–11.

Schlesinger, Sarah. *500 Low-Fat Fruit and Vegetable Recipes.* New York: Villard Books / Random House, Inc., 1992.

Schneider, Elizabeth. *Uncommon Fruits and Vegetables: a Commonsense Guide.* New York: Harper & Row, Publishers, Inc., 1986.

Shepherd, Renee, and Fran Raboff. *More Recipes from a Kitchen Garden.* Berkeley, Ca.: Ten Speed Press, 1995.

_____. *Recipes from a Kitchen Garden.* Berkeley, Ca.: Ten Speed Press, 1993.

Smith, Nancy. "Basil, From Garden to Kitchen." *Back in Thyme,* January 1997, p. 5.

Spitler, Sue. *1,001 Low-Fat Vegetarian Recipes.* Chicago, Il.: Surrey Books, 1997.

Thomas, Anna. *The New Vegetarian Epicure.* New York: Alfred A. Knopf, 1996.

_____. *The Vegetarian Epicure.* New York: Random House, Inc., 1972.

_____. *The Vegetarian Epicure Book Two.* New York: Alfred A. Knopf, 1978.

Toomay, Mindy, and Susann Geiskopf-Hadler. *The Best 125 Meatless Pasta Dishes.* Rocklin, Ca.: Prima Publishing, 1992.

INDEX

PLEASE KEEP IN TOUCH

If you enjoy *Rolling Prairie Cookbook* and would like us to mail extra copies to you, or to your friends as gifts, we'll be happy to do so. Enclose a check or money order payable to Spring Wheat Nutrition Education Services. Cost of each book is $14.95 plus $3.00 shipping and handling. Kansas residents please include an additional 88¢ sales tax per book. Please specify if this is a gift. We will enclose a small gift card. Carefully write out what you would like us to say on the card. All cookbooks are autographed by the author. For information on quantity prices, write or FAX us at the following address.

SEND ORDERS TO:

Spring Wheat Nutrition Education Services
1198 N 700 RD
Lawrence, Kansas 66047
FAX (785) 331-0842

If you would like to be notified of future books, upcoming classes, or publication of our upcoming newsletter *What to Eat*, please write or FAX us at the above address. We would be happy to add you to our mailing list.

NANCY O'CONNOR M.S.Ed. is an author, nutrition educator, and cooking instructor. She received a master's degree in health education from the University of Kansas in 1994. For the past five years she has developed recipes featuring seasonal produce for the Rolling Prairie Farmers Alliance. Currently, she works as a full-time nutrition educator for Community Mercantile Cooperative Grocery in Lawrence, Kansas. Nancy conducts classes and workshops on healthy eating throughout the Midwest. She serves on the board of Ozark Cooperative Warehouse in Fayetteville, Arkansas. Nancy will be publishing a monthly newsletter *What to Eat* featuring healthy recipes and nutrition information. She lives in the country outside Lawrence, Kansas with her husband and two sons.